GIFTS FOR THE GODS

1501

GIFTS FOR THE GODS

ANCIENT EGYPTIAN ANIMAL MUMMIES AND THE BRITISH

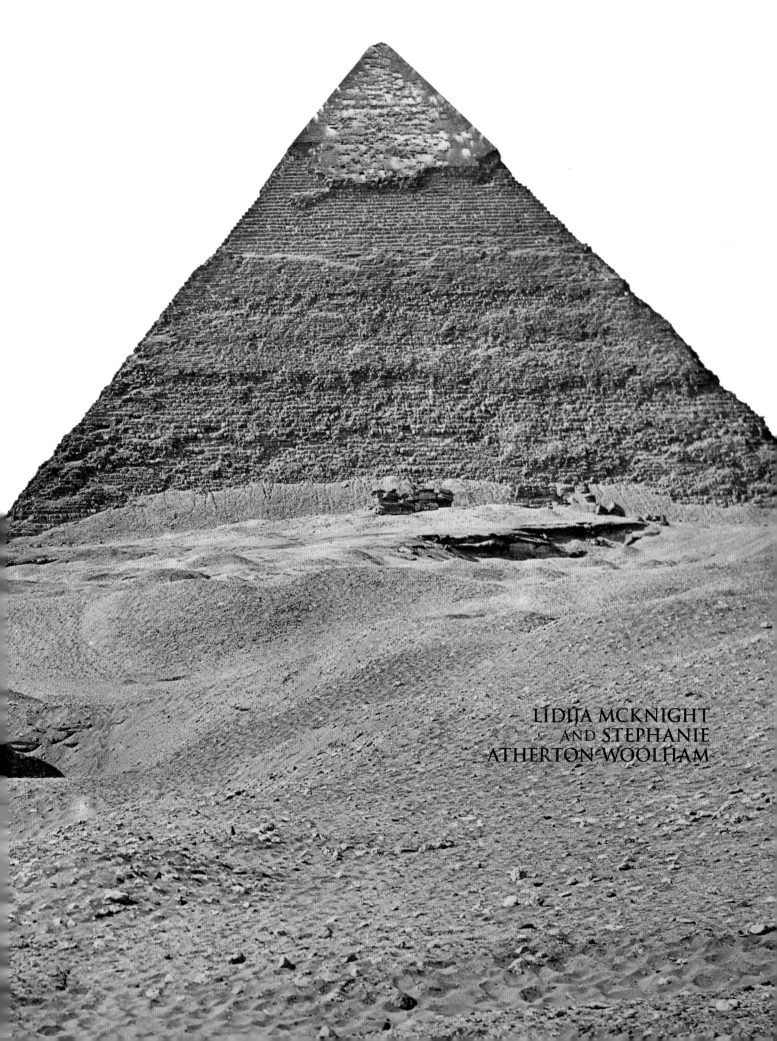

LIDIJA MCKNIGHT
AND STEPHANIE
ATHERTON-WOOLHAM

For Toby Alexander, Amy Sophia
and Blake Christopher

First published 2015 by
Liverpool University Press
4 Cambridge Street
Liverpool
L69 7ZU

British Library Cataloguing-in-Publication data
A British Library CIP record is available

ISBN 978-1-78138-255-4

Designed by Carnegie Book Production
Printed and bound in the UK by Henry Ling Ltd

Cover image: Jackal mummy (Acc. No. EG726, Oriental
Museum, Durham). Reproduced by permission of Durham
University Museums.

Cover background image: Bird pots after excavation
at Saqqara. Reproduced by permission of the Egypt
Exploration Society, London.

The research is supported by The Leverhulme Trust,
the Wellcome Trust and the KNH Charitable Trust.

The Leverhulme Trust

No animals or animal mummies were harmed
in the making of this book.

Contents

Acknowledgements

The editors would like to express sincere thanks to the museums and private institutions, which have supported the project; without their assistance and enthusiasm, the project would not have grown to what it is today. Grateful thanks go to the trustees at the Central Manchester University Hospitals NHS Foundation Trust for access to the radiography suite and the research endowment fund; particularly to Professor Judith Adams, Consultant Radiologist, whose knowledge, time and enthusiasm for the project and the radiographic study of mummified material is inspirational. To the team of dedicated radiographers at the Trust who give their time and expertise to assist in the acquisition of radiographic images, which often involves them staying late into the night. Thanks are extended to our imaging partners, most notably Mr Robert Hill, Consultant Orthopaedic Surgeon, at the Portland Hospital, London.

We would like to thank The Leverhulme Trust (RPG-2013-143) for the significant financial support given to the project since 2010 and the KNH Charitable Trust for continuing assistance. We are grateful to the Wellcome Trust for granting a People Award (WT106317MA) to enable us to design the book's namesake exhibition.

To Alison Welsby, Liverpool University Press, for being there to answer our often absurd queries. To our colleagues Richard Sabin, Joanne Cooper and Judith White, at the Natural History Museum, for their expertise and support of our experimental mummification programme. We extend our thanks to Professor Don Brothwell, University of York, who planted the 'animal mummy' seed in the first place, and to Professors Rosalie David and Andrew Chamberlain, The University of Manchester, for their continued support. Special thanks go to Campbell Price, Joanne Robinson and Katy Turner for their assistance with the editing of this book. To the curatorial and conservation staff at the exhibition host venues – Manchester Museum, Kelvingrove Museum and Art Gallery, Glasgow and World Museum, Liverpool – for their valuable advice and support. To the scholars who have contributed to this book, we are indebted to you for your time, dedication and professionalism.

To our families, friends and colleagues who have put up with more than we ever could have hoped for. To those who asked *what is it that you actually do?* – we hope this book provides the answer. To those who, knowing what we do, asked us *why?* – this one's for you!

Chronology of Ancient Egypt

Dates	Dynasties	Period
5300–3000 BC		Predynastic
3000–2686 BC	1–2	Early Dynastic
2686–2160 BC	3–8	Old Kingdom
2160–2055 BC	9–10 (11 Thebes only)	First Intermediate
2055–1650 BC	11–14	Middle Kingdom
1650–1550 BC	15–17	Second Intermediate
1550–1069 BC	18–20	New Kingdom
1069–664 BC	21–25	Third Intermediate
664–332 BC	26–30 and 2nd Persian	Late Period
332–30 BC	Macedonian and Ptolemaic	Ptolemaic
30 BC–AD 395	Roman	

(Shaw 2000)

Forewords

Mummy studies at The University of Manchester

Prof. Rosalie David, OBE

The Manchester Egyptian Mummy Research Project was established at The University of Manchester in 1973 (David 1979). It aimed to develop a pioneering methodology to investigate Egyptian mummified remains, and to use these scientific techniques to explore causes of death, patterns of disease, diet and lifestyle, mummification techniques, and religious and funerary beliefs in ancient Egypt. Many of the principles and techniques which comprise this 'Manchester Method' have subsequently been adopted by other researchers investigating Egyptian and other mummified remains.

The Manchester team comprised an interdisciplinary group of specialists; the project was initially successful because the various elements required for the study came under the auspices of one supportive authority – The University of Manchester. These requirements included the significant collection of Egyptian mummies held at Manchester Museum (a university facility), and university departments and teaching hospitals that could provide access to extensive scientific resources and equipment.

The project's original focus was human mummies, and the initial research was limited to individual studies of mummified remains held in the Manchester Museum collection. However, early radiological and anatomical studies also included a survey of the museum's animal mummies (David 1979, 13–17). Eventually, the research was expanded to include scientific investigation of collections held in other museums (for example, the Leeds Mummy, see David and Tapp 1992). Techniques have included radiology, palaeohistology, electron micro-scopy, palaeodontology, immunocytochemistry, ancient DNA, radiocarbon dating, mass spectrometry and other instrumental protocols, and the scientific reconstruction of mummified heads (David 2008).

In 1975, the decision was taken to unwrap and autopsy a poorly preserved mummy (Acc. No. 1770) in the Manchester Museum collection; this was the first scientific autopsy of an Egyptian mummy since Dr Margaret Murray's pioneering investigation of the mummies of the 'Two Brothers' in Manchester in 1908 (Murray 1910). Extensive information was derived from the 1975 autopsy, and the preserved remnants provide invaluable material for ongoing research. From 1979, the team promoted and developed virtually non-destructive methods of investigation, utilising the industrial endoscope to obtain tissue samples from inside mummies for histological studies.

In 1995, the team was invited to collaborate with scientists working in Egypt on an epidemiological study on Schistosomiasis. This joint project aimed to construct epidemiological profiles of the disease in ancient and contemporary Egypt, and compare the incidence patterns (Contis and David 1996; Lambert-Zazulak *et al.* 2003). To achieve this, it was necessary to gather data from a large number of individuals, and the International Ancient Egyptian Mummy Tissue Bank was established at Manchester to collect and store samples from mummies in collections around the world. In 2010, the Ancient Egyptian Animal Bio Bank was founded to collate data, images and samples from mummified animal material to bring this neglected field in line with human mummy research.

Animal mummies: a zooarchaeologist's perspective

Prof. Don Brothwell

Victorian travel books recommended that visitors were mindful not to stand downwind whilst animal mummies were being excavated for fertiliser, in view of the dreadful smell. As a zooarchaeologist, my concern relates more to the scientific value of animal mummies, and to welcome this current publication, which forms a worthwhile addition to the limited range of studies on animals in Egypt and Sudan. When considering these specimens, I should really say what 'looks' like a preserved animal body, as some turn out to be anything but. Indeed, in looking at the radiographs of some of these pseudo-mummies, one could be forgiven for thinking of an ancient world filled with rogues and tricksters. The surface of the wrapped mummy may suggest a well preserved bird, cat or crocodile, but the interior may tell a different story. The authors of this book reveal some of the surprises in store for those undertaking such investigations.

Ancient preserved and mummified animals in museum collections around the world continue to hold a macabre fascination for the public and researchers alike. The museum curator is faced with an ethical dilemma: mummies are a finite resource, but more research is needed to enable us to understand their production. Non-destructive methods of investigation such as the use of X-rays, as well as CT scans, are essential, although a micro-sample of tissue enables biomolecular analysis. Animal mummies have been especially neglected in this respect, but the situation is now greatly improving, as exemplified by collections-based reviews of animal mummies such as that of the National Museum of Antiquities in Leiden (Raven and Taconis 2005).

These animals, produced as votive offerings to satisfy religious motivations, can yield important biological information and, as a zooarchaeologist, I seek to answer questions of the physical remains themselves. *Is there evidence of pathology and does it indicate a form of environmental stress? Within a sample of a particular species, is there evidence of inbreeding? If ancient DNA could be extracted successfully, could we reveal close genetic relationships?* From current research, there is no evidence that specimens were selected for abnormality, but of course we need to compare these votive cases with normal zoological specimens. If the votive animals were badly treated in life, or selected for small size or another variable, then this might be revealed by radiography and other comparisons. Keeping wild species in captivity could also result in modified growth or health problems. The techniques at our disposal with which to determine these answers depend on access to the specimens, equipment and, in some cases, on the ability to obtain viable samples.

The authors of this work provide much needed evidence that, whatever the difficulties, much progress can be made in this field of Egyptology. I'm sure I do not need to remind them that beyond the British collection of animal mummies, there are countless others – plenty for a lifetime of research! But they are to be congratulated on the work they have achieved so far.

Prologue

The ancient Egyptians believed that a living being consisted of physical and ethereal elements, which required preservation after death. Of vital importance was the physical body, which was thought to act as a receptacle for the unique aspects that constitute an individual e.g. the soul and personality. Through mummification, the physical body was preserved in a true likeness of the individual in life, which enabled recognition and reunion of the body and ethereal elements after death (Ikram and Dodson 1998, 18; Taylor 2001, 16; Von den Driesch et al. 2006, 236).

A 'mummy' refers to a preserved body consisting of a skeleton with associated soft-tissue, which can be preserved naturally (as a result of environmental conditions, such as with simple pit burials) or artificially (through human intervention). The ancient Egyptians practiced artificial mummification (with varying degrees of success) from the Early Dynastic to the Roman Period (Aufderheide 2003, 25). Most recognise that the ancient Egyptians mummified animals as well as humans, yet few appreciate the sheer volume and variety.

Animal mummies are generally thought to belong to one of four categories – pet, victual (food), cult and votive – based upon their intended purpose and significance to the ancient Egyptians (Ikram 2005). A commonly held misconception is that all animal mummies were pets; although pet mummies do exist, they are relatively rare. Victual mummies are also less well represented in the archaeological record. These mummies, often cuts of meat or prepared fowl, were left as an offering in the deceased's tomb. Cult animals were believed to be living representations of the gods on earth. A single individual was chosen because of certain characteristics or markings, and these high status animals were worshipped in life and death by followers of the cult to which they belonged.

The fourth category, and the one to which we turn our attention in this book, are votive mummies. Intended as 'gifts for the gods' they are by far the largest group and are generally the mummies that we find in British museum collections. Beyond their deposition in enormous subterranean catacombs and their subsequent excavation (many by British explorers and archaeologists), very little is known about how and why they came to be mummified.

Research at The University of Manchester over the past 15 years has studied 800 votive mummies, 600 of which are in British museums with collections ranging in size from one to 80 mummies. In 2010, the Ancient Egyptian Animal Bio Bank project was established to collate information, images, samples and the results of scientific analysis on these animal mummies, reuniting them virtually for the first time since their removal from Egypt in the nineteenth and twentieth centuries. In doing this, a pioneering protocol for animal mummy research has been formulated with the hope of creating a standard by which researchers around the world can approach their study. The Bio Bank has allowed the largest cross-collection and cross-species comparative study of this diverse group of artefacts, to date. Moreover, the Bio Bank continues to grow as more collections join the project.

In this book, academic specialists join us to share some of the lesser-known histories behind British animal mummy collections, and how and why they came to be here. We describe our protocol and the results of the research so far on this enigmatic assemblage, the 'gifts for the gods', to promote understanding of the practice of animal mummification and, ultimately, inspire further mummy research.

Lidija McKnight and
Stephanie Atherton-Woolham

1 Understanding the Landscape and Environment of Ancient Egypt

Everywhere else in the world people live separately from their animals, but animals and humans live together in Egypt...
(Herodotus as translated by Waterfield 1998, 109)

Before investigating animal mummies it is necessary to consider the history of the Egyptian landscape in order to understand how environmental changes affected biodiversity in North Africa. This chapter examines the geological and biological history of the region, making use of ancient Egyptian art and archaeology, alongside museum natural history collections to understand nature's variety in this part of the world.

Fig. 1: Map of Egypt.
Courtesy of Stephanie
Atherton-Woolham.

1.1 Understanding the ancient Egyptian environment, with reference to natural history specimens in museums

Henry McGhie

As a zoologist attempting to understand the historical environment, it is necessary to think about the evidence available to us. Our knowledge of the ancient Egyptian environment is heavily coloured by the culture and artefacts that the civilisation left behind. Looking at these materials, it is important to recognise that the way in which we interpret them is coloured by our own culture. John Berger, the British novelist, argued that animals have gradually disappeared from Western life and that the human-animal relationship has been stretched by nineteenth-century capitalism (1980). With this in mind, it is perhaps not so remarkable that birds and other wildlife feature so heavily in ancient Egyptian thought, but that they occur less frequently in our own culture.

The ancient Egyptians lived in a world of natural symbols and auguries, based on the movements and activities of birds, animals, plants and celestial entities. Separating fact from fiction is, thus, not straightforward. When considering the surviving evidence, we should ask whether the ancient Egyptians intended to represent the reality of nature, an idealised imaginary version, 'supernature', or indeed, something else that we cannot ourselves comprehend. *When presented with images of* Branta ruficollis *(Red-breasted Geese), which would be an extraordinary sight in modern Egypt, are we looking at biological records – in the style of sightings of rare birds by birdwatchers today – or are we looking at something else? Was this an everyday consideration or an extraordinary occurrence? Are we looking at birds that entered Egypt by their own devices or through human trade?* Although many birds and other animals are faithfully represented in art and material culture, we should avoid the assumption, tempting as it might be, that these depictions (however lifelike within the constraints of representational conventions) were intended as direct representations of real places and biological communities.

Of particular interest is the development of 'celebrity' species by the ancient Egyptians, which featured in their art and religious rituals, for example *Threskiornis aethiopicus* (Sacred Ibis). Understanding the reasons behind the development of animal 'celebrity' remains difficult or even impossible to establish. We can presume that the development of such 'celebrity' was influenced by stories told about them,

the status of the people who told the stories and their relationships with other people, in addition to the ways that the stories were woven into the lives of listeners.

Wider investigation of the environment through geology and meteorology shows that Egypt and surrounding regions have experienced dramatic and complex climatic change throughout history (see Wyatt 1.2). It can be inferred that many species associated with more temperate and colder climates (northern and

Fig. 2: The spirit collection store at Manchester Museum. Photo: Lidija McKnight.

Fig. 3: Study skins of *Threskiornis aethiopicus* (Sacred Ibis) (centre) and *Falco biarmicus* (Lanner Falcon). Photo: Alan Seabright. Reproduced by permission of Manchester Museum, The University of Manchester.

upland species) would have spread further south during periods of colder climes, while southern species would have spread further north during warm periods. This simplistic view does not, however, cover the subtlety by which species respond to changes in climate. Firstly, species vary in their ability to deal with environmental variables, such as temperature and humidity; and they vary in their ability to deal with rapid fluctuations of these variables. Secondly, species vary in their mobility, affecting their response to environmental change. Thirdly, a combination of climatic conditions at particular latitudes can generate unexpected, unpredictable and surprising species' communities. For species at the northern and southern limits of their range, migratory behaviour can be dramatically altered, with such species becoming increasingly mobile in the face of environmental change. Given that the ancient Egyptians were keenly aware of the seasonal movement of animals, this is of more value than simple biological interest.

It is, of course, quite wrong to discount the actions of humans from fluctuations in the natural environment, as pressures coming from each source operated simultaneously. Human and environmental pressures also interact: low rainfall could lead to the modification of irrigation systems and watercourses, further reducing local availability of water in times of shortage.

If ancient Egyptian artistic depictions of the environment are open to interpretation, scientific investigation of the abundance of animals and plants that they so diligently preserved, as well as those preserved accidentally, can be called into question. Preserved specimens reveal information on populations, species and biological communities, provided that analyses are undertaken with due consideration of the assumptions regarding the circumstances of their selection and preservation. We should seek to determine the nature of our samples, in much the same way as we would evaluate artistic depictions of the landscape. *Were they randomly selected and, if not, why not? Do the remains really tell us something about the past, or do they tell us more about the people who collected and preserved them?* If we understand the nature of the recorded past, we can use it to explore and interpret the changes that have occurred since.

Museums contain vast stores of preserved specimens from the distant past and from more recent times. The majority of these collections date from the nineteenth and early twentieth centuries, when natural products were acquired, sorted and catalogued in Western museums. Collecting still continues, but at a considerably reduced level. Natural history collections generally consist of mounted animals used for display, scientific specimens known as study skins (which preserve the skin), dried skeletons, and spirit specimens (preserved in alcohol or formaldehyde) (Fig. 2). Each has its particular

Fig. 4: The natural history stores at Manchester Museum showing the variety of taxidermy specimens. Photo: Lidija McKnight.

uses and limitations. Study skins (Fig. 3) were collected to enable people to understand which animals live where, and how they vary from place to place. They usually have good data on their collection locality, but lack their 'contents' (skeleton and soft tissues). The same is true for mounted specimens (Fig. 4), which are less likely to have good quality locality information. Skeletal remains are common in collections but often lack data on origin, sex or condition of the animal; they are more commonly found as single or small samples. Animal mummies (Fig. 5) represent another category of preserved natural history specimens held in museums; however, the primary motivation behind their acquisition stems more from an interest in the civilisation, rather than the animals themselves. The value of these mummified specimens as indicators of the ancient environment and species diversity is highlighted through the application of scientific analyses. 'New' forms of collection include bio-banking facilities, such as the Ancient Egyptian Animal Bio Bank (see McKnight 4.1).

Studies of animal biometrics, disease and growth have historically used study skins and skeletons in museum collections. Scientists now combine these traditional analyses with new methods, which would seem alien to the original collectors. Carbon dating, in widespread use since the 1950s, is used to date specimens and Polymerase Chain Reaction (PCR) enables DNA extraction from very small samples, potentially enabling species identification, and understanding genetic diversity within and between populations. Stable isotope analysis studies proteins in feather, hair, bone and skin and is used to reconstruct the diet and growing conditions of tissues. These techniques provide new avenues of enquiry to explore the natural world.

The discovery of new techniques that could be applied to old specimens is a terrific boon to their usefulness, but there have been drawbacks. Collections of historically important specimens should not be seen just as a 'smash-and-grab' tissue bank, but as a resource to be used responsibly and sustainably. Techniques develop rapidly, so that sample sizes required for DNA extraction, for example, are now much smaller than initial studies required, making their application to museum collections more ethically viable. Collections are often used as a proxy for the natural world; as collections age, however, the reliability of this assumption is increasingly called into question.

The study and comparison of animal remains from ancient and modern Egypt present many exciting research questions. Studies of stable isotopes in feathers have been used to trace the diet and migratory routes of birds, and there may be opportunities to apply such techniques to birds preserved in ancient times (West *et al.* 2006, 2010). Could this type of technique be applied to mummified animals shedding light on their past movements, thereby enabling the reconstruction of ancient migratory routes? In using these techniques, what inherent assumptions would we be making? Could the diet of ibises from the *Ibiotropheia* (ibis feeding places) (Kessler and Nur el-Din 2005, 124; Von den Driesch *et al.* 2006, 203) be revealed through the use of novel techniques? The extraction of DNA from mummified animal remains is still in its infancy and further studies in this regard are needed to perfect the methodology for small samples. Through research projects such as the Ancient Egyptian Animal Bio Bank at The University of Manchester (see 4. Animal Mummy Investigations at Manchester), mummies in museum collections will undoubtedly aid the study of species diversity in ancient Egypt. As a result, insights on the selective breeding and domestication of particular species may be possible. The list of questions is endless; however, with proper attention to the assumptions being made of samples, scientific investigation can be used to explore particular hypotheses.

In a rapidly changing world, understanding species variability and dynamics in the ancient world is of more than academic interest. Thorough understanding of ancient population dynamics can measure the rate of evolution and species turnover. Techniques of investigation have proliferated rapidly over the last 50 years: inconceivable new avenues will likely be available to researchers 50 years from now.

Fig. 5: Animal mummies in the organics store at National Museums Liverpool. Photo: Lidija McKnight.

1.2 Biodiversity in ancient Egypt

John Wyatt

The variety of flora and fauna found within the geographical boundaries of Egypt is great (Baha el-Din 2012; Hoath 2003; Osborn and Osbornova 1998; Wyatt and Garner forthcoming). It is influenced by many aspects including geology, climate, habitat, water availability, and human impact; each bearing an influence on species diversity and the ecosystem. Determining ancient biodiversity requires knowledge of the above aspects, but rather than observing the environment through a pair of binoculars as we would in modern Egypt, we must make use of zooarchaeological, palaeobotanical and Egyptological (namely hieroglyphic and artistic) resources. The limitations of this type of evidence in reaching a positive species identification for the ancient Egyptian landscape should be noted. In particular, in the accuracy of artistic and hieroglyphic depictions, the continued portrayal of species no longer extant at the time of depiction (see McGhie 1.1), and the presence of imported animals and plants.

A clear understanding of the ancient environment (incorporating geology, climate and habitat) is the foundation upon which we can determine biodiversity in ancient Egypt.

Geology

Egypt's geological base (Sampsell 2014) consists of metamorphic and igneous rocks, deposited some 2000–550 billion years ago, which are now exposed at Aswan and the higher mountains of the Eastern Desert and Sinai Peninsula. An intermediate layer of Nubian sandstone was deposited in the Cretaceous Period and this, in turn, was covered from about 95–55 million years ago, by alternating layers of shale and limestone. Nubian sandstone is now exposed in southern Egypt with limestone remaining the surface rock for most of the central part of the country, as far north as Cairo (Fig. 6). Sandstone, shale and limestone are all the result of sedimentation in the ancient Tethys Sea, which repeatedly flooded and exposed much of what is now North Africa.

The Sinai Peninsula is geologically divided into three parts: a metamorphic and igneous mountain massif in the south, a central limestone plateau, and folded limestone hills leading to coastal sand dunes in the north. It provides the only land bridge between the African and Asian continents, and was used by animals such as *Bos primigenius* (Auroch), *Equus asinus* (Wild Ass), *Capra ibex* (Alpine Ibex), *Ammotragus lervia* (Barbary Sheep), and *Hyaena hyaena* (Striped Hyena). These species are thought to have reached Egypt between 126,000–14,000 years ago (Osborn and Osbornova 1998).

Geologically, the River Nile is some six million years old. Two main tributaries form the Nile in Egypt today: primarily the Blue Nile from Lake Tana in Ethiopia, and the White Nile from Lake Victoria (Strouhal 1997, 92). The Ethiopian tributaries joined around 800,000 years ago with its sediment completely filling the massive sandstone and limestone-walled canyon, which existed previously from the Mediterranean southwards to at least Aswan. However, the pre-dammed Nile, with additional water from Central Africa and perennial summer flooding, is much more recent and commenced approximately 12,500 years ago (Said 1981). These sedimentary soils created the fertile Nile Valley farmed by the ancient Egyptians, and were inhabited by a wide variety of flora and fauna, often recorded on temple and tomb walls.

Geography, climate and habitat

It would be easy to consider Egypt's four main geographic areas, the Western and Eastern Deserts, the Sinai Peninsula and the Nile Valley (Fig. 7), as separate macro-habitats that reacted to climate change at exactly the same time and

Fig. 6: Surface limestone in the Western Desert. Photo: John Wyatt.

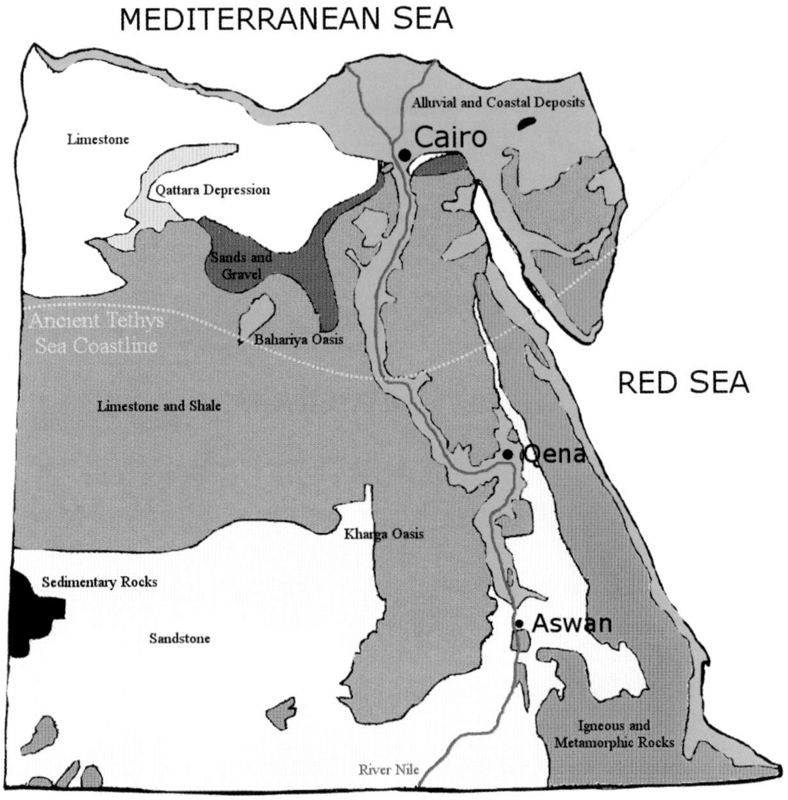

MEDITERRANEAN SEA

Fig. 7: Geological map of Egypt. Courtesy of John Wyatt.

The Sinai Peninsula continues to be the richest of Egypt's geographic areas. The high mountains and proximity to the weather systems of the Red Sea and Mediterranean equate to higher levels of precipitation, in spite of its general aridity. These, in turn, have created a habitat for a diverse range of fauna and flora.

The final, but perhaps most important, area was the Nile Valley. Resident water-seeking animals remained close to its shoreline throughout the year and it was also a stopover for thousands of birds during migration seasons. Large mammals, such as *Loxodonta Africana* (African Bush Elephant), *Diceros bicornis* (Black Rhinoceros) and *Ceratotherium simum* (White Rhinoceros), also frequented the region on feeding forays. *Giraffa camelopardalis* (Giraffe) visited when supplies of acacia trees in the deserts were in short supply. All such species would ultimately have come into contact with the increasing human population in the Nile Valley, and their presence is reflected in tomb scenes, notably at Beni Hasan and Saqqara. All were at risk of being hunted, and those more vulnerable species, large mammals in particular, would have disappeared by the early Old Kingdom. Some species like *Hippopotamus amphibius* (Common Hippopotamus) and *Crocodylus niloticus* (Nile Crocodile) survived much later but eventually disappeared.*

The River Nile's massive associated flood plain and delta, caused by the annual flood recession, produced complex habitats. This phenomenon attracted many wintering wildfowl from Europe, alongside many summer breeders and flood season migrants from elsewhere in Africa. However, the Nile flood was irregular with long periods of both low and high water levels, both of which could be disastrous to humans and wildlife. Historically, periods of low flood were associated with severe civil unrest, such as during the First Intermediate Period. It is becoming clear that high water levels could be just as catastrophic. The destruction of infrastructure in the Nile Delta during the 12th Dynasty (Sampsell 2003, 42) forced pyramid building to move southwards. This resulted in estuarine birds, such as *Tadorna tadorna* (Common Shelduck), to be depicted as far south as Deir el-Bersha (Ray, personal communication; Wyatt and Garner forthcoming) (Fig. 8).

in exactly the same way. The reality is that climatic conditions throughout the country were arid between 38,000–8,000 BC. However, a shift in the Earth's orbit allowed the equatorial conditions of Central Africa to rapidly extend northwards. Enhanced summer rains and moist savannah-type vegetation accompanied this phenomenon.

Desiccation began to return from *c.* 4,000 BC, which is thought to have started in the Western Desert. Pastoralists living on Egypt's disappearing grasslands were forced to move, with their animals, to the oases and in close proximity to the Nile to find food and water. Wild animals, including *Addax nasomaculatus* (Addax) and *Oryx dammah* (Scimitar-horned Oryx), were forced to do the same, coming into competition with man for territory and water. Only species independent of water, such as *Fennecus zerda* (Fennec Fox), would have survived in the desert. Rock art in the Eastern Desert however, suggests that desertification, alongside major human activity, began approximately 500 years later than in the Western Desert. The Red Sea monsoons, some seasonal water and the local weather conditions created by the Desert's mountains, were responsible for this delay and the continued presence of species such as *Litocranius walleri* (Gerenuk) into the Predynastic Period.

---

* Both have, however, now returned to Lake Nasser.

Howard Carter
1893.

Fig. 8: Detail from Howard
Carter's painting of
the great clap-trapping
scene from the Tomb
of Djehutyhotep at
Deir el-Bersha showing
Tadorna tadorna (Common
Shelduck). © Griffith
Institute, University of
Oxford.

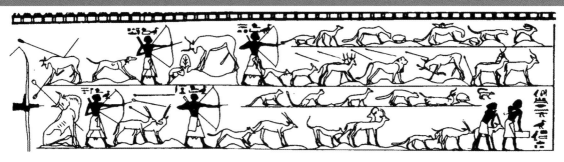

Fig. 9: Details of a great variety of species from two desert hunting scenes from the Tombs of Baqt III and Khnumhotep II at Beni Hasan. Reproduced by permission of the Egypt Exploration Society, London.

Zooarchaeological and Egyptological evidence, to date, has identified 150–60 mammalian species (Osborn and Osbornova 1998; Wyatt and Garner forthcoming).* Approximately 243 bird species have been identified, but of these some 40 no longer occur, even as vagrants (Wyatt and Garner forthcoming) (Fig. 9). In addition, some 42 possible fish species (Brewer and Friedman 1989), as well as 85 reptilian and 8 amphibian species, have been identified.

Levels of biodiversity in ancient Egypt began to decline during the Pharaonic Period, with human impact being the predominant causative factor. The effects of climate change, desertification and habitat loss contributed to this decline, and continue to do so to this day.

---

* 21 species had disappeared by the Dynastic Period, whilst a further 12 became extinct during Pharaonic rule and 15 more since 395 AD.

2 Divine Donations: Gifts for the Gods

*The dedication of votive objects
in sacred areas such as temples,
shrines, and cemeteries was an
optional practice for which there is
sporadic archaeological evidence...*
(Pinch and Waraksa, 2009, 2)

The same concept of 'gifting' occurs today in Western society, usually under the auspices of religious request or thanksgiving. From the simple act of lighting a candle in a church, to the deposition of memorial tributes at the site of a tragedy, offering a votive is still common human behaviour. This chapter addresses how and why animal mummies were used as votive offerings in ancient Egypt.

Fig. 10: Bronze
statuette of Osiris, with
dedication on base:
'May Osiris give life (to)
Djedbastetiuefankh, son
of Padikhonsu, his mother
is Herybastet'. Donated
in 1867 by Joseph Mayer,
provenance unknown
(Acc. No. M13519, World
Museum Liverpool).
Reproduced by permission
of National Museums
Liverpool, World Museum.

2.1 Votive practice in ancient Egypt

Campbell Price

Fig. 11: Wooden shrine containing bronze votive images of gods, still wrapped in linen, as found at the Sacred Animal Necropolis, Saqqara. Reproduced by permission of the Egypt Exploration Society, London.

The Egyptian gods, it seems, were very demanding. They required constant attention in the form of perpetual temple ritual, a major component of which was the presentation of a range of offerings that were expected to satisfy divine appetites, as they might sate human ones. Yet, the gods also appear to have been relatively easily placated, with the gifting of objects being an obvious form of appeasement. Although it is only ever the king who is depicted as giving offerings to the gods on temple walls, the reality of such pious action encompassed all of society.

Many objects that have survived from Pharaonic Egypt can be interpreted as gifts to the gods (Pinch and Waraksa 2009). Those associated with animal cults during the first millennium BC survive in abundance; a testament both to the scale and longevity of such votive practice.* These objects most often take the form of images of the gods themselves, appealing perhaps to a divine sense of vanity. The giving of votives was a materialised form of prayer, physically marking an appeal or an expression of thanks. The durability of metal – as opposed to more perishable tokens, though these do occasionally survive – and the careful collection and deposition of votive bronzes, rendered these intentions permanent, to the eternal benefit of deity and donor.

---

* I use the term 'votive', while acknowledging that it can be problematic as it presupposes a purpose and viewpoint; I define a 'votive object' as anything donated to a god in hope of divine response.

It may be significant that earlier New Kingdom votive practice appears to have a focus on the cult of the goddess Hathor (Pinch 1993), whose animal manifestation – that of a cow – had particular popular appeal. Bronze images of deities from the first millennium BC survive in comparable numbers to the millions of animal mummies with which they are closely connected. The portability of both these types of object is a reflection of their ancient ease of sale and dedication, and a reason for their wide modern distribution as museum objects. Sadly, this has resulted in a lack of sure provenance for most votive animal mummies and bronzes, leading in turn to a general lack of synthesised study (Schulz 2004, 61–6).

It is a particular characteristic of Egyptian monuments (including small objects) that their texts emphasise their intended function. Be they large stone statues or small votive bronzes, all are in some sense dedications to impress the gods. Hieroglyphic script ('divine words') was targeted as much at a readership among the gods as by human beings; to some extent it was immaterial whether inscriptions were seen and read, or not, for the dedication to 'work'.

Bronzes, because of their small size, do not usually bear extensive texts explaining their purpose (De Meulenaere 1990, 63–81). Any inscription is mostly limited to a short caption of favourable intent; the gift of 'life' is most commonly mentioned (Fig. 10), echoing the non-material benefits that the king receives from the gods on temple walls (Schulz 2004, 62). Specific titles are rare and in many cases only the name of the donor is recorded (Davies 2007, 184), though this should not create an undue impression of a broad social spectrum of donors; all but the crudest bronzes cannot have been cheap (Baines 2000, 44–6).

Many of those votive bronzes found *in situ*, such as those from the Sacred Animal Necropolis at Saqqara (Fig. 11), retain evidence of having been wrapped in linen (Zivie and Lichtenberg 2005, 109, fig. 5.3; Davies 2007, 180, fig. 77). Such wrapping was of considerable cultural significance (Riggs 2014, 136–8) and emphasises the conceptual link between the votive bronzes and animal mummies: both are physical forms of the divine – eternal images, shrouded in linen to maintain and enhance their sacredness.

Some hollow bronze images of gods even contain small amounts of mummified material, illustrating the blurring between categories of 'votive'. For example, a bronze statuette of a lioness-headed goddess – Sekhmet or Wadjit – now in Plymouth City Museum and Art Gallery, preserves linen remains in the cavity of its seat (Fig. 12). While the mummified fauna in the cavities in the bases of falcon statuettes have been suggested as food for the gods represented by the statuette (Smith 1974, 54), the animal remains (of any species) may have been thought to enhance the power of the figure itself.

The occasion of offering the bronze votives is nowhere explicitly recorded, but these are not likely to have been formal, prescribed rituals but rather *ad hoc*, at the convenience of individuals or family groups (Eyre 2013, 113), perhaps especially at festivals (Davies 2007, 184–5). The gathering together of votives *en masse* for permanent deposition in caches is likely to have mirrored the practice of collecting and depositing animal mummies. This recalls again the similarity in the basic intention of both votive bronzes and animal mummies: to act as a conduit between the divine and a human supplicant, and to permanently mark – and thus make more efficacious – the pious act of donation.

Fig. 12: Bronze statuette of a lioness-headed goddess, with mummified material in the seat cavity (TWCMS: 2001: 406, Plymouth Museum and Art Gallery) Photo: Lidija McKnight.

2.2 Animals as votive offerings in ancient Egypt

Stephanie Atherton-Woolham and Lidija McKnight

Whilst animals in Predynastic Egyptian imagery 'represented manifestations of power' (Silverman 1991, 13) to a predominantly illiterate population, they also acted as symbols from which people could draw strength, courage and hope. In addition, they represented specific geographic areas acting in the same way as a totem (Kessler 1986, 574), thus protecting the locality in which the image resided. These localities later developed into administrative provinces, or nomes, and continued to be represented by these symbols, which were often animals (Fig. 13) (Butzer 1976, 61). Frequently the animal in question represented the natural landscape of the nome itself. The worship of Sobek for instance was predominantly found in the

Fig. 13: Nome gods at the temple of Edfu. Photo: Stephanie Atherton-Woolham.

Faiyum region; an area particularly suited to the Nile crocodile, his sacred animal, where the Bahr Yusef and Lake Moeris provided a plentiful water supply.

Later visitors to Egypt, notably the ancient Greeks and Romans, recorded the unusual degree of reverence by the ancient Egyptians towards their animal world (Bleiberg 2013, 63–105). Herodotus, in particular, wrote that the ancient Egyptians 'prayed' to animals because of their divine association, and that it was a punishable offence to harm certain living animals (Teeter 2002, 335; Waterfield 1998, 121). Indeed, such theories developed during

the Middle Ages (and into the modern era) with the concept that every cat in ancient Egypt was worshipped as a result of the combined emotions of fear and love on the part of the Egyptian population (Zivie and Lichtenberg 2005, 106). Our own, modern attitudes are also partly responsible for the continued lack of understanding about the role of animals in ancient Egypt (see McKnight and Price 3.1). The mass mummification and burial of animals such as cats, dogs, fish and birds in ancient Egypt, many of which are now considered pets, confuses our understanding of the meaning and purpose of votive animal mummies.

To a certain extent, theories regarding the divine status of animals are valid, although a more accurate interpretation would be to say that the gods chose to 'install' (Assmann 2001, 43) themselves in an image of divine capabilities. Such images acted as avatars for the divine essence of the god, and included live and mummified animals alongside man-made images of the gods in their animal, or human-animal, composite forms (see Price 2.1). It should be noted however that the *god* was the focal point for worship, channelled through an image taking the form of their respective sacred animal (Meeks and Favard-Meeks 1996, 30). This provided a focus for divine responses to prayers, dream interpretations and oracular enquiries (Kessler 1986, 573–4; Teeter 2011, 76; Zivie and Lichtenberg 2005, 106).

Millions of votive animal mummies date to the Late-Roman Periods (*c.* 664 BC–AD 395) (Kessler and Nur el-Din 2005, 155–6; Nicholson 2005, 49; Zivie and Lichtenberg 2005, 107). Archaeological and literary evidence suggests that Tuna el-Gebel was the first *ibiotapheion* (ibis burial place) to be established in Egypt and was likely given such status by royal decree during the reigns of Psamtik I (664–610 BC) and Amasis (570–526 BC) (Kessler and Nur el-Din 2005, 124; Von den Driesch *et al.* 2006, 203). Tuna el-Gebel was a major focus of the ibis cult, maintained for a period of 700 years by priests and not, apparently, by pilgrims (Von den Driesch *et al.* 2006, 203), with ceremonial activity overseen, for safety, by a military escort (Kessler and Nur el-Din 2005, 124–5). The purpose of such burial places and their practices was thought to represent a sense of nationalistic pride, in terms of their beliefs and traditions, during foreign rule (Nicholson 2005, 49); and a way by which the gods could be appeased (see Price 2.1). The financial and legal support from foreign rulers implies an understanding of the significance of the ancient Egyptian belief system, and its crucial role for the country's political and economic stability (Kessler and Nur el-Din 2005, 127–9; Von den Driesch *et al.* 2006, 241).

By the Ptolemaic Period, local necropoleis appeared across Egypt to deal with the mummification and burial of *all* sacred animals within their locality (Kessler and Nur el-Din 2005, 142). At Saqqara, species-specific subterranean catacombs for animal mummies were constructed and filled with the offerings of pilgrims (see Nicholson 3.4). An animal mummy could be purchased to act as a divine messenger for their particular ailment or problem, delivered to their intended god by temple staff in the hope of a divine response (Bleiberg *et al.* 2013; Ikram 2005). It was still tradition, however, that special temple animals were buried in their historical locality (Kessler and Nur el-Din 2005, 126).

The acquisition of animals for votive mummification

Our understanding of the means by which animals were acquired for votive mummification in ancient Egypt is limited. There is no definitive textual or archaeological evidence relating specifically to this mechanism; however, several theories exist.

Textual evidence for *ibiotropheia* (ibis breeding places) during the Late-Roman Periods is known (Drew-Bear 1979), with several in the Hermopolite nome where Tuna el-Gebel is located. These places were natural areas capable of sustaining a mixed population of farmed and wild animals (Kessler and Nur el-Din 2005, 142).

Archaeologically, some have been identified, including the Hod Tuna, a now dry biotope, at Tuna el-Gebel (Von den Driesch *et al.* 2006, 204–5); 'the lake of Pharaoh' at Saqqara (Nicholson 2005, 48; Ray 1978, 153); and a sacred lake at Hermopolis Parva (Friedman and Buck 2008). It is without doubt that such areas were not restricted to a single species; the presence of water encouraged plant life, which in turn

provided shelter. Food was provided by both temple staff (Ray 1976, 139), and also by the natural landscape in the form of vegetation, insects and small mammals. Indeed, zooarchaeological evidence demonstrates that species diversity was great (see 1. Understanding the Landscape and Environment of Ancient Egypt), although not every animal necessarily had sacred connotations to a particular god. *Ibiotropheia* were an important part of the sacred landscape associated with temples and the gods that resided within them, therefore any creature that lived, and died, within this area was deemed sacred by association, and thus worthy of mummification and rejuvenation (Von den Driesch *et al.* 2006, 238). Textual evidence supporting this concept is seen in a Demotic inscription on a coffin from the Falcon Catacomb at Saqqara, which describes the collection of a deceased hawk found within the temple enclosure, which was subsequently mummified and buried (Ray 2011, 271–3).

Evidence is apparent for human involvement in the rearing of animals as votive offerings. At Medinet Maadi in the Faiyum, a nursery area for crocodiles was excavated connected to a small basin, likely for water, where the hatchlings were thought to congregate after birth. It was thought that a number lived in this area adjacent to the temple before dispatch and mummification (Bresciani 2005, 204–5). In addition, at Saqqara, an area designated block 3, sector 7 was thought to be a hatchery for ibises and falcons. The remains of eggshells found in terracotta jars, alongside high walls, indicate that this area may have functioned as an incubation area (Martin 1981, 27). Ostraca carrying a bird 'stamp' found in the same locality further emphasised this building's possible function (Ray 1970). The question remains as to how eggs and young animals came into the possession of temple staff. They may have been collected by local crocodile, ibis and falcon cult servants for rearing within the temple complex, rather than in an *ibiotropheia* or in the wild. Perhaps these individuals were part of 'sacred populations' who resided (and died) within the temple complex and, upon death, their mummified remains were ceremonially used (Kessler and Nur el-Din 2005, 125–6).

3 Egypt and the British: Archaeologists, Collectors and Collections

It may be said of some very old places, as of some very old books, that they are destined to be forever new. The nearer we approach them, the more remote they seem; the more we study them, the more we have yet to learn. Time augments rather than diminishes their everlasting novelty; and to our descendants of a thousand years hence it may safely be predicted that they will be even more fascinating than to ourselves. This is true of many ancient lands, but of no place is it so true as of Egypt.

(Edwards 1891, 3)

The British have played an important role in the discovery, excavation, recovery, purchase and distribution of animal mummies. Many animal mummies held in museum collections today came to Britain via agents who visited Egypt in the nineteenth and twentieth centuries. In this chapter, we explore how some of the most notable individuals influenced collecting habits of their time, and how their legacy has shaped British museum collections.

3.1 Early British fascination with Egypt

Lidija McKnight and Campbell Price

[I]t would hardly be respectable, on one's return from Egypt, to present oneself in Europe without a mummy in one hand and a crocodile in the other.

*(European monk, 1883.
Quoted in Fagan 1975, 11–13.)*

Ancient Egypt has, it seems, always held a special allure for the West. From the curiosity of ancient Greeks and Romans through to modern sightseers, Egypt is seen as an exotic treasure house filled with endless mysteries. Early British fascination with ancient Egypt was intertwined with political ambitions. After the defeat of Egyptian-Sudanese forces by the British in 1882, Egypt became a British 'protectorate' enabling the British Empire to considerably increase its influence in this strategic part of the world. This created a unique link between the North African country and the European super-power.

To wealthy British socialites of the nineteenth century, Egypt represented the ideal travel destination. They could experience the wonders of an ancient civilisation, enjoy a warm climate to cure ills brought on by the inclement British weather, and collect tales and mementos with which to impress family and friends upon their return (Fig. 14). It is through the surviving memoirs of early travellers that we learn much about the attitudes towards the people and customs of both ancient and modern Egypt. Personal accounts echo, yet also contrast with, romantic orientalising depictions of Egypt in nineteenth-century paintings (De Meulenaere 1992) (Figs 15 and 16). Monumental sculpture and inscriptions were highly prized, yet these were very expensive to procure and unwieldy to transport (Fig. 17). Acquisition of such impressive antiquities was largely the privilege of national governments who competed to stock state museums. Mummies, however, were relatively easy to come by at this time and embodied many perceptions of Egypt as a strange, eternal, yet somehow familiar land.

The custom of purchasing mummies as souvenirs sparked a trend for 'mummy unrollings' (Fig. 18), popular in eighteenth- and nineteenth-century Britain (Moshenska 2014, 451–77). Interestingly, although these events were destructive acts largely staged as entertainment, those conducting the theatrical 'performance' were often trained clinicians, well-versed in human anatomy and respected in their fields. The audience may not have necessarily understood what they were witnessing, but the person wielding the scalpel invariably claimed to; so although the resulting destruction of irreplaceable artefacts would be considered unforgivable to modern eyes, at the time it represented the best that scientific mummy studies could offer.

Fig. 14: Tourists climbing the Great Pyramid, 1870s–80s. Reproduced by permission of Manchester Museum, The University of Manchester.

Fig. 15: *Sacred to Pasht*, 1888, Edwin Longsden Long. Reproduced with the kind permission of the Russell-Cotes Art Gallery and Museum, Bournemouth.

Despite their relative abundance, human mummies still posed logistical challenges for a traveller, as the Macclesfield heiress Marianne Brocklehurst describes during her 1873–4 trip along the Nile: the mummy she purchased was too much of an inconvenience to take home (Brocklehurst 2004, 107–16). In contrast, an animal mummy was the ultimate portable curio; a little piece of ancient Egypt that would fit neatly into a trunk for shipment to Britain, especially at a time when it was popular to hunt the living relatives of mummified species (Fig. 19). Even the famous explorer and show-man Giovanni Battista Belzoni performed the 'unrolling' of a mummified monkey (Anon. 1821, 342). Many animal mummies in British museums left Egypt with such travellers, were installed in their homes as talking points and objects of fascination, before being donated to museums as philanthropic acts by their owners, or bequeathed upon death by surviving relatives who found little use for them.

One such traveller was William Wilde (1815–76), Irish surgeon and father to eminent writer and poet Oscar Wilde (Fig. 20). With a keen passion for archaeology, William travelled extensively in Egypt from the 1830s, publish-ing his travel memoirs as *Narrative of a Voyage to Madeira, Tenerife, and along the shores of the Mediterranean* in 1840. His account is typical of nineteenth-century adventurer-travellers and documents Egypt at first hand, describing the people he met and the spectacles he witnessed. Particular attention is drawn to the catacombs at the site of Saqqara:

> At length we arrived at where we
> could stand upright, and creeping
> over a vast pile of pots, and sinking
> in the dust of thousands of animals,
> we came to where we felt the urns
> still undisturbed, and piled up in
> rows with the larger end pointing
> outwards.
>
> (Wilde 1840, 390)

Fig. 16: *Alethe Attendant of the Sacred Ibis in the Temple of Isis at Memphis*, 1888, Edwin Longsden Long. Reproduced with the kind permission of the Russell-Cotes Art Gallery and Museum, Bournemouth.

Fig. 17: *Mode in which the young Memnon's Head (now in the British Museum) was removed* (Belzoni, 1820). Photo: Neil Douglas. Reproduced by permission of the Portico Library, Manchester.

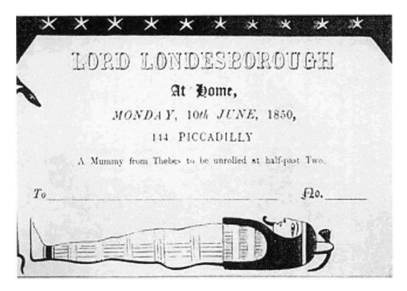

LORD LONDESBOROUGH

At Home,

MONDAY, 10th JUNE, 1850,

144 PICCADILLY

A Mummy from Thebes to be unrolled at half-past Two.

To _____ No. _____

Fig. 18: The invitation issued by Lord Londesborough to the unrolling of a mummy at his home in 1850.

is it ?   no it is'nt !   yes it is !!!

OUR FIRST CROCODILE

Fig. 19: Illustration from the diary of Marianne Brocklehurst, drawn in Spring 1874. The party was returning north through Lower Nubia searching for crocodiles, whilst her nephew, Alfred, remained in the boat with his gun. Reproduced with permission from the Silk Heritage Trust, Macclesfield.

Fig. 20: Portrait of William Wilde.

He even mentions comparing ibis bones from the catacombs with some zoological specimens:

> In the museum of the school of medicine at Cairo, I had an opportunity of seeing and comparing both the black and the white ibis with the bones of those found in the mummy-pits at Sackara [sic] ... Great heat must have been employed in the preparation of these mummies, as the majority of them are so much roasted, as to crumble to dust on being opened.

(Wilde 1840, 464)

Sadly, we do not know the current whereabouts of the six ibis pots mentioned in Wilde's memoir. Despite this, like that of many early travellers, his account is immensely evocative, fuelled by the magic and mystery of ancient Egypt, and the quest to report on the riches of its civilisation for the benefit of a Western readership.

3.2 'The Father of Egyptology'? Flinders Petrie and animal mummies

Alice Stevenson

The ubiquity of animal mummies in museum collections across the world has often been observed (Ikram 2005, xv). It is therefore perhaps surprising to note then that University College London's Petrie Museum of Egyptian Archaeology has relatively few (Fig. 21). In total there are approximately 15 complete, or partially complete, mummified animals accessioned into the collection and all are votive mummies (Ikram 2003, 235). These bundles of bone, skin and linen were acquired at different times and with different appreciations as to their value for understanding the past. One of the first to be obtained by University College may have predated W. M. Flinders Petrie's (Fig. 22) appointment to the first Chair of Egyptian Archaeology and Philology in 1892 by some 63 years: records in UCL show that a cat mummy was presented to the University Council by Sir

Fig. 21: Ibis mummy (Acc. No. UC.30690), Petrie Museum of Egyptian Archaeology. Reproduced with permission from UCL Petrie Museum of Egyptian Archaeology.

Anthony Panizzi in 1829, most likely as a 'wondrous curiosity' (Moser 2006). Of the remaining examples in the Petrie Museum today, only the crocodile remains can be firmly attributed to excavations directed by Petrie, by which time new frames of reference informed their place within museum collections.

Petrie's teams encountered numerous mummified animals on his excavations, including crocodile remains at Hawara (Petrie 1889, 10) and Lahun (Petrie *et al.* 1923, 39); several species of birds and mammals at Dendereh (1900, 59); and cats at both Abydos (1902, 39) and Gizeh (1907) (Figs 23 and 24). Despite his reputation as an archaeological innovator, Petrie, like many individuals in the late nineteenth and early twentieth century, seems to have regarded animal mummies as having only limited archaeological and artefactual value (Ikram

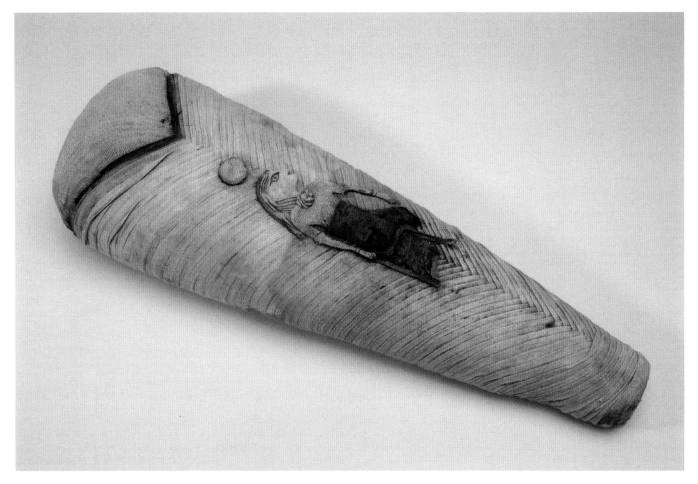

2005, 1). For Petrie, the archaeological object was one that was informed by provenance and date, because 'a specimen may be inferior to others already in a museum, and yet it will be worth more than all of them if it has a history' (Petrie 1888, vii). However, many of the specimens from Petrie's excavations that found their way into institutions around the world – from the United States to Cape Town (Cornelius *et al.* 2012) – are often frustratingly silent as to their original provenance and date, denying them that history (Armitage and Clutton-Brock 1981, 188). Similarly, animal mummies are notably absent from his distribution lists of finds and from his notebook entries. Petrie's diaries, the originals of which are kept today in the Griffith Institute, Oxford, make passing mention to the vast numbers of crocodiles recovered at Hawara, but also the disappointment that so few antiquities accompanied them. This sentiment was reiterated by his colleagues whose own interests in animal mummies were aroused only by the papyri with which they were entangled (Grenfell *et al.* 1902, vi).

Petrie himself wrote little on the subject, save for a few brief allusions to ancient Egyptian cult practice (Petrie 1912). Nevertheless, he did send faunal specimens to colleagues for scientific analysis, like Oldfield Thomas of the British Museum (the former Natural History section). Thomas provided species identifications that were reported in Petrie's excavation memoirs, although they were not incorporated into discussion or synthesis of the sites (Petrie 1900, 59–60; 1907, 29). Such initiatives, therefore, appear to be less related to Petrie's own efforts to understand ancient Egyptian history and practices, and more dependent upon the research interests of fellow scientists, whom he perhaps knew through London's professional societies, or else through social encounters in Egypt where those with means often wintered. For example, from the mass of animal remains from Dendereh, selected specimens were 'handed to the Natural History Museum at South Kensington, where they are being elaborately studied in connection with Dr Anderson's work on the Egyptian fauna' (Petrie 1898, 29; cf. Anderson 1898).

In summary, in Petrie's day the study of sacred animal remains was bound up with standard Victorian taxonomic and classificatory enterprises, rather than interpretive efforts to understand the techniques of ancient embalming or their meaning. Thus, although Petrie was a central figure in the creation of what constituted an archaeological artefact, this did not extend to animal mummies. These remained ontologically separate zoological specimens, removed from the processes of archaeological contextualisation and interpretation. The recognition that animal mummies were cultural artefacts that were crafted and representational (Riggs 2014, 89) was beyond Petrie's time.

Fig. 22: Photograph of Flinders Petrie in his mid to late 30s (1885–1890). Reproduced with permission from UCL Petrie Museum of Egyptian Archaeology.

Fig. 23: Signed photograph of Flinders Petrie from the Amsden Collection. Reproduced with permission from UCL Petrie Museum of Egyptian Archaeology.

Fig. 24: Photograph of Flinders Petrie on excavation, possibly in Memphis in 1910. Reproduced with permission from UCL Petrie Museum of Egyptian Archaeology.

3.3 The British at Abydos, Egypt: the contributions of T. Eric Peet and W. Leonard S. Loat to the study of animal cemeteries

Rozenn Bailleul-LeSuer

In his book dedicated to the Upper Egyptian site of Abydos, O'Connor (2009, 9) stated that, 'as the burial place of Egypt's earliest historical kings, and subsequently as the major cult centre, literally over millennia, for the god Osiris, ruler of the dead, Abydos' place in Egyptian history is of extraordinary significance'. This religious prominence did not fade during the later periods of Egyptian history. The discovery of multiple animal burials scattered throughout the sacred landscape of Abydos bears testimony to the involvement of the local priesthood in various sacred animal cults, whose popularity soared during the Ptolemaic and Roman Periods. The presence of these animal cemeteries was first brought to light by British archaeologists T. Eric Peet and W. Leonard S. Loat working under the aegis of the Egypt Exploration Fund (EEF), now known as the Egypt Exploration Society (EES).

Whereas the first attempts at clearing Abydos' temples and cemeteries had started in 1859 with Auguste Mariette, it was W. M. Flinders Petrie's well-organised excavation programme which prompted the EEF, in 1899, to sponsor a British presence at such a notable site, which continued until the onset of World War I (Kemp 1982, 71–2). The first major animal cemetery was reported during this period by Peet, working at the time under the leadership of Edouard Naville (Fig. 25). In 1910, he unexpectedly uncovered a dogs' hypogeum, which he described as being

> a complex of underground chambers
> … cut in the solid rock. [...] Each
> chamber, and even the long corridor
> which connects them, is filled to
> within 1.50 metres of the roof with
> a mass of mummified animals piled
> in orderly rows one above the other.
> [...] The vast majority of mummies,
> of which there must be many thou-
> sands, seem to be those of dogs...[*]
> (Naville and Peet 1910–11, 4–5).

A few years later, during the fifth season at Abydos, a second burial site for animals emerged from the sand during the excavation of the necropolis overlooking the processional way leading to Umm el-Qa'ab, named 'Nécropole du Centre,' or Middle Cemetery, by Mariette (1880, 40). A section of this cemetery, labelled cemetery E by Peet, was assigned to Loat for excavation. Loat had started his career in Egypt as a naturalist by carrying out an ichthyological survey of the Nile and by studying the local avifauna, before joining the EEF team of archaeologists working at Gurob and later at Abydos (Dawson and Uphill 1995, 258). The ibis cemetery unearthed in the midst of human burials in cemetery E gave him the opportunity to combine both his expertise as an ornithologist and as an archaeologist. In *The Times* of 20 February 1913, he provided this detailed account of his discovery.[†]

> In another part of the site has been
> found a cemetery of ibises, where
> thousands of these sacred birds
> were buried in the Roman period in
> large jars just below the surface of
> the desert sand. Many of the birds
> had been mummified with extraor-
> dinary care, the outer wrappings
> consisting of narrow strips of linen
> in two colours, white and black,
> accurately arranged in exquisite
> geometrical patterns. Some of these
> mummies proved, when unwrapped,
> to contain only feathers of the ibis,
> which were evidently collected with
> great care as belonging to the sacred
> bird. Even the eggs were regarded
> as sacred, and several of the jars
> contained specimens of them, which
> are still intact. Other birds, such as
> hawks, were found in the cemetery,
> together with rare examples of oxen,
> sheep, dogs, shrews, and snakes.
> This cemetery, taken in conjunc-
> tion with the dogs' catacomb found
> in 1910, shows that in the Roman
> period Abydos had assumed a great
> importance as a burying ground for
> sacred animals.

Fig. 25: Long line of workers excavating the entrance to the dogs' hypogeum under the supervision of several field directors, possibly including Edouard Naville and T. Eric Peet. Reproduced by permission of the Egypt Exploration Society, London.

---

[*] See Peet (1914, 99–102) for a description of the dog catacombs, and Haddon (1914, 40–48) for the analysis of a small sample of dog mummies collected in these galleries.

[†] Excerpt from 'Egypt Exploration Fund. Work at Abydos'. *The Times*, London. Published on Thursday, 20 February 1913, 9.

Fig. 26: Selection of well-preserved 'ibis' mummies discovered in cemetery E by W. Leonard S. Loat displaying bicoloured linen wrappings arranged in a coffered design. Reproduced by permission of the Egypt Exploration Society, London.

Loat (1913, 40–7) proceeded to examine and record all the animals recovered during this season (Fig. 26). He systematically reviewed the contents of the 93 large clay vessels discovered under the drift sand (Fig. 27), as well as the skeletal remains of oxen, sheep and dogs found enclosed in small brick structures at the base of several jars (Fig. 28). While the best preserved mummified bundles* were kept intact and sent to the various institutions financing the expedition, the other mummies were systematically unwrapped and dissected.

The involvement of Britain in the armed conflict of World War I in August 1914 prevented Peet and Loat from pursuing their work at Abydos. Both joined the army, Peet serving with the King's Liverpool Regiment and Loat in the Garrison Artillery (Tutton 1932). American archaeologist Thomas Whittemore (1914, 248–9) led the excavation that year and further reported on this section of cemetery E.

Animal mummies continue to this day to be regularly uncovered at Abydos (Ikram 2007, 2013); yet the work conducted by Peet and Loat in the ibis cemetery remains an invaluable resource. A selection of the mummies sent by the EEF to the financing museums and institutes is now the object of study and has recently been incorporated into The University of Manchester's Ancient Egyptian Animal Bio Bank. The authors of this book are thus, a century later, pursuing the work of their compatriots.

---

* Only a limited number of animal mummies were found with their wrappings intact. In a letter dated 3 September 1913 and addressed to J. H. Breasted, director of the Oriental Institute at the University of Chicago, Thomas Whittemore, writing on behalf of the EEF, reported that 'of the 1,500 ibises from the ibis cemetery at Abydos, hardly more than forty were considered in a condition sufficiently sound to warrant their being packed at all, and of these many suffered irreparably in their transportation to London.' Courtesy of the Oriental Institute of the University of Chicago.

Fig. 27: View of the ibis cemetery at Abydos. In the foreground, a thick layer of drift sand had been removed, exposing several large clay vessels filled with animal remains. Reproduced by permission of the Egypt Exploration Society, London.

Fig. 28: Bovid skull unearthed in a brick enclosure at the base of one of the large jars. Reproduced by permission of the Egypt Exploration Society, London.

3.4 British work at the Sacred Animal Necropolis, North Saqqara, Egypt

Paul T. Nicholson

Although what we now call the Sacred Animal Necropolis at North Saqqara (Fig. 29) is popularly thought of as a discovery of the Napoleonic expedition (*Description* Tome V Pl.1 and Pl.4) or to have come to light with Mariette's discovery of the Serapeum in 1851 (Mariette 1857),* it was already well known at a much earlier date.

The 'pits' or 'wells' of the birds were established as visitor attractions at least as early as the eighteenth century. One of the earliest accounts by a Briton is that by Richard Pococke (1704–65) who published an account in 1743, including a sketch of part of one of the bird catacombs (Pococke 1743) (Fig. 30). However, these monuments, so attractive to the adventurous early travellers, became less popular later in the nineteenth century as a result of mass tourism introduced to Egypt by Thomas Cook in 1869. The 'ibis mummy pits' still featured in Murray's (1888, 268) *Handbook for Travellers* but by that date they were little visited and did not warrant inclusion on his map. By the early twentieth century the 'bird pits' were all but forgotten about and their location was lost, only coming to prominence again through the work of Professor W. B. Emery (1903–71) in the 1960s.[†]

Modern archaeological work at the Sacred Animal Necropolis

On 5 October 1964, Emery began excavations on behalf of the Egypt Exploration Society 'in the valley area at the extreme west of the archaic necropolis at North Saqqara' (Emery 1965a, 3) (Fig. 31). His primary aim was not to begin a new phase of work on the cults of sacred animals, but rather to try to 'discover the Asklepieion and the tomb of Imhotep, the great architect and vizier of King Zoser...' (Emery 1965a, 3). This focus on Imhotep immediately led to international interest and popular press coverage (Emery 1965b; Bacon 1967a, b, c). The area of his work was strewn with pottery of the Ptolemaic and Roman Periods in a way which reminded him of the Umm el-Qaab at Abydos (Emery 1965a, 3).

He was well aware of the strangeness of finding 'remains of this late period in an area devoted almost exclusively to monuments of the first five dynasties... [which] suggested at once a place of pilgrimage' (Emery 1965a, 3). Whilst the pilgrimage he envisaged was to the tomb of Imhotep, who had become deified during the Late-Ptolemaic Periods (Hart 1986, 99; Wilkinson 2003, 112), his work actually made clear the great scale of the animal cults at Saqqara and their role in popular pilgrimage. Emery did not find the tomb of Imhotep, though it may be the large uninscribed mastaba number 3518 (Wilkinson 2003, 112).

Initial excavations revealed a large catacomb of mummified ibis in pots and stacked

Fig. 29: Map of North Saqqara showing the location of the animal catacombs. Drawing: Joanne Hodges. Reproduced by permission of P. T. Nicholson.

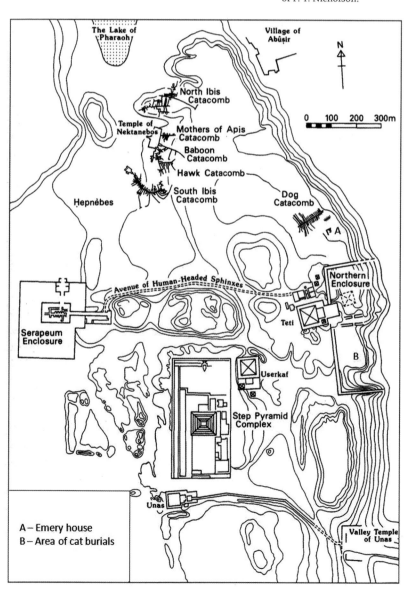

A – Emery house
B – Area of cat burials

---

* This is a summary publication of the work. For others see Dodson (2005).

† I am indebted to Professor H. S. Smith for his comments regarding Emery's work and for reading a draft of this paper.

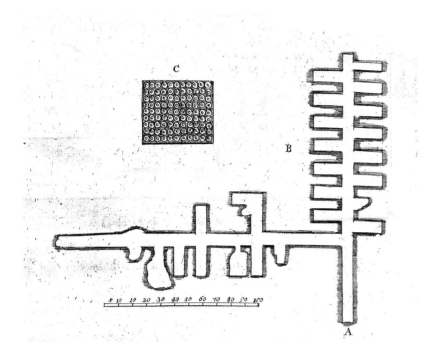

Fig. 30: Extract from Richard Pococke's sketch of part of one of the bird catacombs as published in his *A Description of the East and Some Other Countries*, 1743. His 'A' is the location of one shaft entrance while 'B' seems to be another shaft entrance. 'C' shows the stacked pots at the end of one of the galleries, or 'apartments' as he describes them.

from floor to ceiling in a series of side galleries opening from a main axial corridor. Graffiti in the galleries showed that it had been one of the places visited by early travellers (Martin 1981, 3). In clearing the courtyard outside this catacomb* Emery's team unearthed a hoard of Demotic texts on potsherds written by a temple resident named Hor and dating to the mid-second century BC. These were published as *The Archive of Hor* (Ray 1976). The *Archive* provides extremely valuable historical evidence as well as information on the operation of the ibis cult itself. It appears that there was only one mass burial event per year, the mummies being gradually accumulated in a *house of waiting*, a feature which requires further research (Ray 1976, 140). The Emery expedition noted that sometimes mummy pots were found either empty or containing little but bones, or at the other extreme that two or more mummies might be placed in a single vessel. This seemed to indicate some kind of sharp practice on the part of the priests and is alluded to in the phrase *wꜥ ntr n wꜣt mgt* 'one god in one vessel' (Ray 1976, 143), a ruling designed to end such an abuse. This collection of texts is the best source thus far known for our understanding of how the cult at Saqqara

---

* The catacomb subsequently became known as the South Ibis Catacomb in order to differentiate from the North Ibis Catacomb which was found in the 1970–71 season. The ostraca were found in two groups, the first in 1965–6 and the second in 1971–2. Hor is sometimes referred to as a priest but the term 'resident' is more accurate.

functioned and may be used, with due caution, to help understand how some of the other animal cults at the site may have operated.

The 1966–7 season saw clearance of part of the Temple Terrace (Fig. 32) and the discovery of clues suggesting that the burial place of the Mothers of Apis cows must be nearby (Emery 1967). The search for these, employing more than 400 workmen (Emery 1969, 31) failed to unearth the entrance to the catacomb during the 1968 season. The 1968–9 season therefore began with the hope of finding the entrance.

However, in December 1968, while clearing along the edge of the escarpment behind the temple terrace, a much smaller entrance than expected was unearthed (Emery 1970, 7). This proved to be the doorway to the Baboon Catacomb. By late January 1969 this was sufficiently clear for the team to discover that there was a break between it and what was at the time believed to be a new ibis catacomb (Emery 1970, 9), but which subsequent analysis showed to be a catacomb of hawks or falcons. Again the cow galleries proved elusive.

The 1969–70 season saw Emery and his team, including some 250 workmen, beginning work in the Falcon Catacomb and also to its north along the escarpment. This work was rewarded on 9 February 1970, with the discovery of the hitherto elusive catacomb of the Mothers of Apis (Emery 1971, 9).

In October 1970 Emery returned to Saqqara (Smith 1971, 201) to continue work on the Mothers of Apis and to prospect further. His efforts led to the discovery of what has become known as the North Ibis Catacomb. However, on 7 March 1971, Emery was found collapsed at the camp and died on 11 March (Smith 1971, 201).

Emery's untimely death brought to an end the main thrust of excavation work at the Sacred Animal Necropolis, although his work was carefully and professionally concluded by Professor G. T. Martin in 1971–2 and 1972–3 (Martin 1973; 1974) and Professor H. S. Smith in 1974–5 (Smith 1974; 1976; Smith and Jeffreys 1977) working on a smaller scale. The work on the Southern Dependencies of the Main Temple Complex was published by Martin in 1981. Fieldwork was transferred in 1976 to the site of the Anubis temple complex (see below). Research and publication of the mass of finds and texts made by Emery and his team has continued to the present day and now comprises 15 large volumes (four site reports, two object catalogues and nine textual publications). In the 1990s, further fieldwork directed by Nicholson was begun to complete aspects of Emery's work,

Fig. 31: Professor
W. B. Emery and his
team of local workmen
clearing the area of the
Temple Terrace, 1965–66.
Reproduced by permission
of the Egypt Exploration
Society, London.

Fig. 32: Aerial photograph of North
Saqqara showing the location of the
findings made by Emery. The image
appeared in the *Journal of Egyptian
Archaeology* for 1965. Reproduced by
permission of the Egypt Exploration
Society, London.

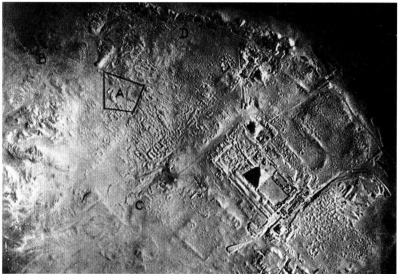

Fig. 33: Kenneth J. Frazer
(1913–2012) took part
in Professor Emery's
expeditions to Saqqara
as well as working with
Professor Smith. In the
1990s he returned to
Saqqara to work with
Nicholson and Smith and
is seen here on the Temple
Terrace during the 1994–5
season. Photograph:
P. T. Nicholson.
Reproduced by permission
of the Egypt Exploration
Society, London.

which required additional information to bring publication to modern standards.

This new phase of work began in 1991 and was greatly assisted by the presence of Mr Kenneth J. Frazer (1914–2012) who had worked with Emery and Smith previously (Fig. 33). Professor Smith, Susan Davies and Ken Frazer concentrated on the Falcon Catacomb and the Mothers of Apis Catacomb, as well as on the Temple Terrace. Nicholson, assisted by Caroline Jackson and Nick Fieller, worked on the mummy pots from the Falcon Catacomb and began to add to, and amend, the preliminary plan which had been made by Frazer of the North Ibis Catacomb (Fig. 34).

This new work has resulted in a number of publications, on the Falcon Catacomb (Davies and Smith 2005), on the Mother of Apis and Baboon Catacombs (Davies 2006) and on the Main Temple Complex (Smith *et al.* 2006). The report on the North Ibis Catacomb is in preparation by Nicholson.

Amongst the results from the renewed work is a greater appreciation of the scale of the cults. Preliminary work by statistician Nick Fieller suggests that the South Ibis Catacomb held some 750,000 mummies, the North Ibis Catacomb about 1,000,000 and the Falcon Catacomb 500,000. The great majority of these are believed to have been donated by pilgrims to Saqqara, making it both a significant centre of personal piety and an important part of both the local and national economy.

Emery's work had concentrated on the west side of the plateau because it was there that he believed the Asklepion and the tomb of Imhotep were most likely to be found. However, the animal cemetery is also present to the east

and it is here that the most recent phase of work began in 2009 with a project to examine the dog catacombs (Nicholson *et al.* 2013; Nicholson *et al.* 2015). The site is not a new discovery, indeed it features on the *Carte de la Nécropole de la Memphite* (De Morgan 1897) and may have been known for some time before that date. Like the catacombs on the west it is associated with a temple (Jeffreys and Smith 1988) and, like them, it is not isolated – there are cat burials and an associated temple immediately to the south which have been investigated by a French team (Zivie and Lichtenberg 2005).

This new work has shown that, like the bird cults, the dogs were a focus of popular religion and it is estimated that some 8,000,000 may have been buried in the larger of the two dog catacombs (Ikram et al. 2013). The study has also been able to throw up interesting parallels with the catacombs on the west and will help to inform the publication of the North Ibis Catacomb.

Conclusion

British excavations – particularly those of Emery – were responsible for bringing the Sacred Animal Necropolis to the notice of the public. However, this interest slipped away following Emery's death and has been revived by the publications of his work by Smith and Davies, and by a renewed interest in personal religion and the place of animals in ancient Egypt. It is hoped that the North Ibis Catacomb can be published in the near future so concluding the publication of the work by Emery, and that the publication of the Dog Catacomb will continue the increasing interest in these two long neglected catacombs.

Fig. 34: Dr. Caroline Jackson working on the extended survey of the North Ibis Catacomb in December 1995. Photograph: P. T. Nicholson. Reproduced by permission of the Egypt Exploration Society, London.

3.5 Unearthing mummified cats, fish and 'monkeys': John Garstang's excavations in the Nile Valley

Anna Garnett

From 1901 to 1909 John Garstang, Professor of the Methods and Practice of Archaeology at the University of Liverpool, directed fieldwork at major Nile Valley sites including Abydos (Snape 1985, 1994), Beni Hasan (Garstang 1907a; Orel 1997), Esna (Downes 1974) and Hierakonpolis (Adams 1987, 1995) on behalf of Liverpool's Institute of Archaeology (now the School of Archaeology, Classics and Egyptology, University of Liverpool). Many of the objects Garstang excavated from his fieldwork in Egypt, Sudan, the Levant and Anatolia, together with the documentary and photographic archive of the excavations, are now kept within the Garstang Museum of Archaeology (Fig. 35).

Garstang assembled 'Excavation Committees' of wealthy private individuals who provided funds to support his fieldwork and, in return, would receive a selection of objects from the excavations. Members of these committees often subsequently donated, sold or gave away their collections, meaning that objects from Garstang's excavations are scattered in museums and private collections around the world, with a particular concentration in the northwest of England (Garnett *et al.* 2011) (Fig. 36). After the Garstang Museum of Archaeology, World Museum Liverpool holds the largest collection of material excavated by Garstang in Egypt and Sudan, much of which entered their collection as gifts from Garstang himself or from the University of Liverpool (see Cooke 3.7).

The need for Garstang to provide high-quality objects for his financial backers is perhaps one of the reasons why he focused mainly on the excavation of cemetery sites since they were more likely to yield fine objects. However, based on extant documentation, the presence of mummified animals at these cemetery sites was relatively limited – as are Garstang's descriptions of them.

From his excavations at Beni Hasan from 1902–4, for example, Garstang records the discovery of a 'plain wooden coffin containing remains of a jackal' (Tomb 17), and in his publication of his excavations at the Late Period cemeteries at Speos Artemidos, near Beni Hasan, he states:

> *The tendency to animal worship was rapidly growing, or throwing off its disguise, and is illustrated here and there by objects found within these graves. The mummied monkey encased in a painted cartonage [sic] in the form of an Osiris … is an illustration.*
>
> (Garstang 1907a, 207) (Fig 37)

Fig. 35: Garstang's workroom inside a rock-cut tomb at Beni Hasan, showing him seated to the right. Reproduced by permission of the KNH Centre for Biomedical Egyptology, The University of Manchester.

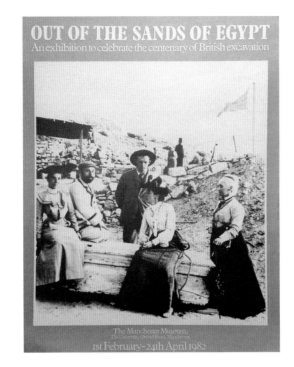

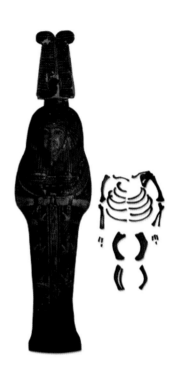

Fig. 36: Poster from an exhibition at Manchester Museum in 1982 depicting Garstang and a party of visitors to his excavations at Beni Hasan. Reproduced by permission of Manchester Museum, The University of Manchester.

Fig. 37: 'Mummied monkey' as described by Garstang in *The Burial Customs of Ancient Egypt* (1907a, 204) (left). Cartonnage and skeletal remains of an infant showing the effects of *osteogenesis imperfecta* (Acc. No. EA 41603, British Museum) (right) © Trustees of the British Museum.

However, this was an unfortunate misidentification: this cartonnage in fact contained the bones of an infant who suffered from the rare disorder *osteogenesis imperfecta*, also known as brittle bone disease. The cartonnage and the skeletal remains are now in the collection of the British Museum (EA 41603) and act as reminders of the importance of using scientific investigation to re-evaluate past interpretations.

In the publication of his work at Beni Hasan, Garstang goes on to mention the discovery in 1889 of a nearby catacomb containing around 180,000 mummified cats at Speos Artemidos (auctioned off at Liverpool the following year) (see Cooke 3.7) and the burial of mummified fish at Esna, where he excavated from 1905–6:

> [From the 25th Dynasty onwards], such cults took definite and local forms, illustrated at Beni Hassan [sic] by the cemetery of cats lying only half a mile distant, and elsewhere in Egypt by the careful interment of every living creature, as, for instance, in the so-called Fish Cemetery at Esna.
>
> (Garstang 1907a, 207)

One such 'careful interment' of a mummified *Lates Niloticus* (Nile Perch), probably excavated by Garstang from this so-called 'Fish Cemetery' at Esna, is now housed at the World Museum Liverpool (Acc. No. 16.11.06.158) (Fig. 38). Garstang worked at Abydos from 1906–9 and in 1907 excavated a Graeco-Roman necropolis in the area of the Great Wadi, which he records yielded mummified hawks (Abdallah 1992, 1–16; Snape 1985, 55). A mummified hawk donated to Kendal Museum by John Rankin – treasurer of Garstang's excavation committee for several years – may originally be from this site (Acc. No. KMA 1993.250; Garnett 2015). Garstang also excavated a chamber tomb at Abydos in 1909 (Tomb 983), reused in the Ptolemaic Period, which he records contained '[?] mummified cats' as part of a small burial assemblage (Snape 1985, 372).

Research into the dispersal of Garstang objects in Britain and beyond, including the on-going reconciliation of objects and archives (Garnett *et al.* 2011; Garnett 2015), facilitates the reconstruction of scattered object groups and continues to increase our understanding of Garstang's contribution to the early development of Egyptology. More, as yet unknown, collections containing mummified animals excavated by Garstang may also become apparent over time, enabling further scientific research and increasing our understanding of the Egyptians' 'tendency to animal worship' in the Nile Valley.

Fig. 38: Group of
mummified animals
excavated by Garstang
from Esna during the
1905–6 season, including
the mummy of a fish
(upper left) likely to have
been from the so-called
'Fish Cemetery' (Acc.
No. 16.11.06.158, World
Museum Liverpool).
Reproduced by permission
of National Museums
Liverpool, World Museum.

3.6 Sir John Gardner Wilkinson and the collection of Egyptian antiquities at Harrow School

Dear Sir ... I shall be most happy if my collection should prove useful in drawing the attention of some of the young Harrovians to those objects in it which may tend to illustrate the customs of old times

(Extract from a letter from Sir John Gardner Wilkinson to Montagu Butler, Head Master of Harrow, 19 September 1864).

John Gardner Wilkinson (Fig. 39) was born on 5 October 1797. He was the son of the Rev. J. Wilkinson of Hardendale, Westmorland (a Fellow of the Society of Antiquaries of London and member of the African Exploration Society), and Mary Anne Gardner Wilkinson. Mary taught her child the basics of French, Latin and Greek before he even began his formal schooling and encouraged the young boy to draw. His early years with his parents, who, having moved to Chelsea, kept company with scholars and travellers, instilled in him a lifelong love of learning, languages, exploration and drawing. His greatest treat was to be allowed to look at his father's learned journals. Following the death of his mother when he was six, and that of his father when he was eight, he was raised by a family friend, the Rev. Dr Yates, chaplain of Chelsea

College. Yates' ambition for the boy was for him to enter the Church. However, when Wilkinson was sent to Harrow in 1813, aged 16, he quickly became attracted to classical studies, to developing his drawing and sketching skills, to the lectures of visiting academics, and the particular scholarly interests of the inspirational Head Master, the Very Rev'd George Butler. This included investigations into understanding the meaning of ancient Egyptian hieroglyphs. These Harrow experiences were formative. Wilkinson decided that on completion of his University career he would apply for a commission in the army because of the opportunities it would afford for travel and exploration. It was at this point that he abandoned any notion of seeking a living in the Church.

In 1816, after completing seven terms at Harrow, he went to Exeter College, Oxford, where he made a number of friends and contacts who were to play a significant part in influencing his future career. During these student years, and not forgetting his Harrow associations, he kept up with the prolific writings of Byron. Wilkinson passed his Final examinations, but never took a degree.

After his 21st birthday and waiting for his commission into the Fourteenth Light Dragoons, Wilkinson embarked on what was then considered a necessary part of any gentleman's education – a Grand Tour Expedition of the Continent. He had already spent summer vacations sketching in Belgium, France and Spain, so now, supported by the modest income he had inherited from his father, he decided to visit Italy. It was this decision that was to change the direction of his life.

Setting off in June 1819 his itinerary took him to Paris, then to Germany and Switzerland, where he practised his newly acquired skills of surveying and mapmaking – skills he believed would be useful in his military career, but were also invaluable for a topographical antiquarian. He filled several notebooks with his observations, about which he was so passionate that he even sketched on horseback so as not to miss any useful reference. He entered Italy in February 1820. The ruins in Rome affected him greatly and he drew them obsessively, comparing his work with classical accounts and immersing himself in the archaeology of the ancient city.

Fig. 39: Photograph of a portrait engraving of Sir John Gardner Wilkinson, given by him to Harrow School in 1864. Reproduced by kind permission of the Keepers and Governors of Harrow School.

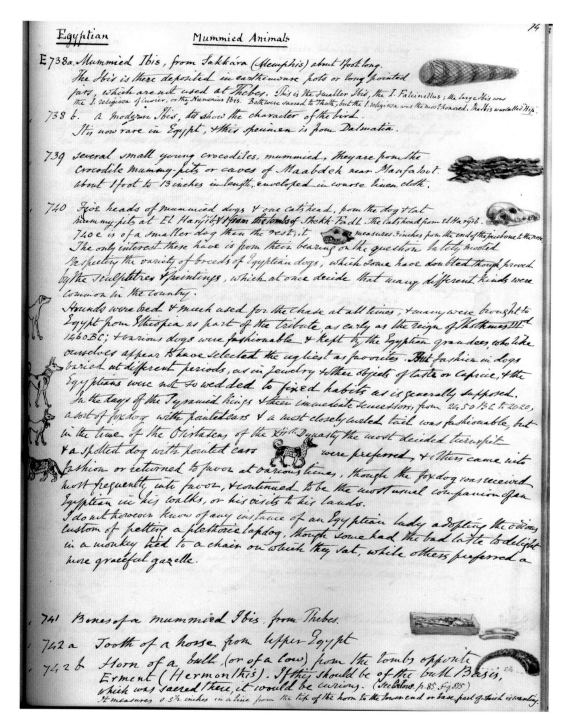

E 738a. Mummied Ibis, from Sakkára (Memphis) about 1 foot long.
The Ibis is there deposited in earthenware pots or long pointed
jars, which are not used at Thebes. This is the smaller Ibis, the I. Falcinellus; the large Ibis was
the I. religiosa of Cuvier, or the Numenius 1819. Both were sacred to Thoth, but the I. religiosa was the most honored. The Ibis was called Hip.

738 b. a modern Ibis, to show the character of the bird.
It is now rare in Egypt, & this specimen is from Dalmatia.

739 Several small young crocodiles, mummied, they are from the
Crocodile Mummy-pits or caves of Maabdeh near Manfalout.
about 1 foot to 13 inches in length, enveloped in coarse linen cloth.

740 Five heads of mummied dogs, & one cat's head, from the dog & cat
mummy-pits at El Harïjé, & from the tombs of Sheikh-Fadl. The Cat's head from El Harïjé
740 e is of a smaller dog than the rest; it measures 3 inches from the end of the jawbone to the nose
The only interest these have is from their bearing on the question lately mooted
respecting the variety of breeds of Egyptian dogs, which I once have doubted though proved
by the sculptures & paintings, which at once decide that many different kinds were
common in the country.
Hounds were bred & much used for the chase at all times, & many were brought to
Egypt from Ethiopia as part of the tribute, as early as the reign of Thothmes III
1460 BC; & various dogs were fashionable & kept by the Egyptian grandees, who like
ourselves appear to have selected the ugliest as favorites. But fashion in dogs
varied at different periods, as in jewelry & other objects of taste or caprice, & the
Egyptians were not so wedded to fixed habits as is generally supposed.
In the days of the Pyramid kings & their immediate successors, from 2450 BC to 2020,
a sort of fox-dog with pointed ears & a most closely curled tail was fashionable, but
in the time of the Osirtasens of the XII Dynasty the most decided turnspit
& a spotted dog with pointed ears were preferred, & others came into
fashion or returned to favor at various times, though the fox-dog was received
most frequently into favor, & continued to be the most usual companion of an
Egyptian in his walks, or his visits to his lands.
I do not however know of any instance of an Egyptian lady adopting the odious
custom of petting a plethoric lapdog, though some had the bad taste to delight
in a monkey tied to a chair on which they sat, while others preferred a
more graceful gazelle.

741 Bones of a mummied Ibis, from Thebes.

742 a Tooth of a horse from Upper Egypt

742 b Horn of a bull (or of a cow) from the tombs opposite
Erment (Hermonthis). If they should be of the bull Basis,
which was sacred there, it would be curious. (Strabo p.85. Fig.815)
It measures 0.5½ inches in a line from the tip of the horn to the lower end or base part of which is wanting.

Fig. 40: Page from Wilkinson's journal describing his observations and showing hand-drawn sketches of the animal mummies he purchased in Egypt. Reproduced by kind permission of the Keepers and Governors of Harrow School.

It was in Rome that Wilkinson was introduced to Sir William Gell, Fellow of the Royal Society – 'Classic Gell', a person much admired by Byron – who was a topographical scholar of some renown and with houses both in Rome and Naples. Gell, 20 years his senior, took to him immediately, recognising a kindred spirit, and gave him access to his maps, books, home and circle of friends, many of whom were distinguished travellers familiar with the ancient sites of the classical world.

Wilkinson left Rome intending to return to England to pursue his commission, but while in Geneva happened to meet up with James Samuel Wiggett, a friend from Oxford, also travelling on a Grand Tour. The two decided, there and then, to become travelling companions with the intention of travelling to Egypt (the military commission evidently no longer a factor), which was, by this time, a safe territory for British visitors, following the defeat of Napoleon's forces in 1801. The pair travelled south to Naples, where

Fig. 41: Ibis mummy (Acc. No. 1864 HE.21, Old Speech Room Gallery, Harrow) illustrated in Wilkinson's journal. Photo: Lidija McKnight.

Gell was now in residence, and accompanied him on a visit to the excavations at Pompeii.* It was here in Naples that they met James Burton, a student of Egyptian hieroglyphs, who would, within a year, receive a commission to work as a mineralogist in the Geological Survey of Egypt. Gell took the opportunity to teach Wilkinson the rudiments of Egyptology during the visit and persuaded him to make ancient Egypt the subject of a major study. The three young men decided they would rendezvous in Cairo and make their expeditions in Egypt together.

Thus, in 1821 Wilkinson arrived in Egypt. He was assisted greatly by the British consul-general in Cairo, Henry Salt, who had been in post since 1815 and whose advice proved invaluable. Wilkinson swiftly adopted full Turkish dress, which made travelling around the country less problematic. Salt's personal interests in archaeology, topography and collecting antiquities made him an ideal mentor; he knew the locations of all the archaeological developments and Wilkinson had already studied all the French publications about Egypt from the scientific studies made under Napoleon. He followed Gell's instructions as to which ancient monuments to visit making accurate notes, sketches and copying inscriptions. He accompanied Salt to the pyramids at Giza and took measurements. His approach was systematic and scholarly. He filled numerous notebooks with his observations, including sketches of the animal mummies he purchased (Fig. 40). He noted errors in published books. In January 1822 he saw his first crocodile and observed

that its lower jaw was not fixed – as Herodotus had described. He journeyed to Thebes, Karnak, Esna, Edfu, Kom Ombo, Aswan, Elephantine and Semna. He visited the crocodile grotto of Maabdah and witnessed the annual rise of the Nile in Nubia. He despatched his companion, James Wiggett, back to Gell in Naples to deliver his drawings of Karnak and, on return to Cairo, determined to focus his area of study on the ancient language of Egypt by copying the inscriptions on the ancient monuments (Shaw and Nicholson 1995; Thompson 1992).

Wilkinson remained in the country for some twelve years, sharing accommodation with Burton on occasion, avoiding the company of other European settlers, travelling, drawing, surveying, excavating, researching, writing and collecting. He understood the importance to archaeology of recording provenance and so his excavations were meticulously and accurately recorded. Today he is mostly remembered for his antiquarian work, but he devoted a good deal of his time to documenting the manners and customs of the people he encountered. In 1837 he published *Manners and Customs of the Ancient Egyptians*, which was so well received that he was given a knighthood two years later (Wilkinson 1994). He never forgot the education he received at Harrow and how the disciplines he learned there enabled him to carve such a distinctive career for himself. It is not surprising that he is referred to as the Father of British Egyptology and inspired the generation of Harrow schoolboys that included British archaeologist Arthur Evans (1851–1941). Evans was just 14 when Wilkinson was in correspondence with the School about the manner in which his antiquities collection should be displayed. The acquisition of the collection, comprising almost one thousand Egyptian objects (Fig. 41) along with dozens of superb Greek, Etruscan and Roman artefacts (Shaw 2008), left a lasting impression on the young Evans. Indeed, in 1873 it was Evans who catalogued Wilkinson's coin collection.

---

*   Interestingly, on Wilkinson's visit to the Museum in Naples he remarked upon an ancient Greek vase depicting the death of Priam, painted by the Kleophrades Painter (Gaunt 2005). Later in life, when he was collecting Greek vases, he purchased from Sotheby's, for 16 shillings, a neck amphora with twisted handles decorated on each side by a satyr, by the self same Painter. He would not have been aware of the association.

3.7 Auctions and air raids: Liverpool's animal mummy collection

Ashley Cooke

World Museum Liverpool originated as the Derby Museum of the Borough of Liverpool in 1853 and was overwhelmingly a museum of natural history, until 1867 when Joseph Mayer (1803–86) adjusted the balance with his donation of 14,000 antiquities and art treasures. The Liverpool Free Public Museum, as it was then known, became England's most important collection of Egyptology after the British Museum (Edwards 1888, 129). However, disaster struck during the enemy air raids of World War II and the museum was destroyed by fire. Few animal mummies from the nineteenth-century donations remain, and the 48 acquired after 1941 reflect the broader acquisition policy of the museum, actively seeking sources nationwide to replenish the collection. As objects they tell a tale of social history, providing snapshots of British interest in Egypt over two centuries, featuring major figures in Victorian collecting and the novel use of cat mummies as fertiliser.

A train arrived in Liverpool from Edinburgh on 13 April 1861, bringing with it the museum's first collection of Egyptology. Around 200 antiquities were purchased for the new museum by William Crosfield (1838–1909), a soap manufacturer, from Rev. Dr Hermann Philip (1813–82), a medical missionary who made visits to Egypt in the 1850s. Philip had his own museum in Gayfield Square, Edinburgh, but in 1861 relocation to Jaffa caused him to sell his collection. Philip's wife packed up the material in three crates and wrote a note advising against unrolling the seven animal mummies in case they 'fall to pieces'; perhaps speaking from some experience. Four ibis mummies, two of which are still in pottery jars, are recorded as being from 'the Ibis Tomb' at Saqqara, still then part of a tourist's itinerary in the mid-nineteenth century (see Nicholson 3.4). But it was not a visit to Egypt that inspired the museum's principal donor to become one of the most important figures in Victorian collecting – he never actually went there. It was the new Egyptian galleries of the British Museum that inspired the goldsmith and jeweller, Joseph Mayer, to establish his own 'Egyptian Museum' in Colquitt Street, Liverpool, in 1852 (Fig. 42). He had always been a passionate collector and now, as a successful businessman, he could buy existing collections wholesale, ensuring their survival for the nation (Gibson and Wright 1988; Yallop

2011, 189–253). Mayer's mission was to inspire the townsmen of Liverpool and to place a study collection within reach of scholars to 'serve as a ground-work for those who are desirous of seeing the high state of civilisation which the Egyptians had attained near four thousand years ago' (Mayer 1852, 2). The first visitors to the museum would have seen 17 animal mummies within 'The Mummy Room', with an adult dog mummy acknowledged as a rarity in the catalogue, 'probably of some highly-favoured and much respected animal, it being very uncommon to find the dog embalmed' (Mayer 1852, 14). Mayer obtained the mummies from Joseph Sams (1784–1860), a bookseller from Darlington. In 1832, Sams had swapped selling books for trading antiquities and went to Egypt and Palestine to gather stock. Some of his collection was sold to the British Museum in 1834. Additions were made to the remainder, and in 1839 Sams exhibited his collection in London and issued an illustrated catalogue to further promote it to prospective buyers (Sams 1839).

The collection included objects collected by Charles Bogaert (1791–1875) of Bruges, many obtained from Jean-Baptiste de Lescluze (1780–1858), a Belgian ship-owner whose collection

Fig. 42: Poster advertising Joseph Mayer's 'Egyptian Museum' in Colquitt Street, Liverpool, 1852. Reproduced by permission of National Museums Liverpool, World Museum.

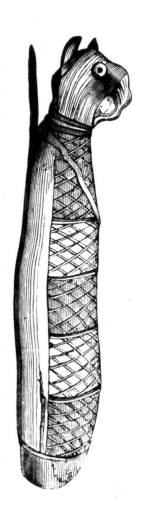

was acquired for Leiden Museum in the late 1820s (De Meulenaere 1993). On the final page of Bogaert's collection inventory is 'une superbe momie avec son chat' (Van de Walle 1976, 56); later this would be regarded as Mayer's finest cat mummy, unfortunately lost in 1941 (Fig. 43). Sams purchased over 100 lots at the sale of Henry Salt's (1780–1827) collection in 1835 but he did not buy lot 1207, 'an ibis and an Epervier mummied, well preserved', the only animal mummies to appear in the printed list of 1270 lots (Sotheby and Son 1835, 98). This suggests Sams was not short of animal mummies and the ones he sold to Mayer may well have been part of the original group he brought back to England in 1833.

Mayer continued to make additions to his Egyptian Museum, buying the bulk of the collection formed by Lord Valentia (1770–1844) in December 1852, mainly obtained from Salt between 1817–20, the British consul-general in Egypt (Dawson and Uphill 1972, 10; 258). Valentia's collection gave Mayer a splendid metre long crocodile mummy that he displayed alongside a large mounted crocodile caught in the Nile around 1850, hung on the wall of 'The Mummy Room' (Fig. 44). X-rays taken in 1995 for the exhibition *Caught in Time* at the Conservation Centre, Liverpool, reveal there are infant crocodiles riding on the back of the adult.

After Mayer's collection came to the museum in 1867, it was confined to three rooms, and curators complained it could not be displayed in a manner which its great value and historical interest required. Ten years later an extension gave the curator, Charles Gatty (1851–1928), an opportunity to create a new Egyptian gallery, accompanied by an illustrated catalogue. Animal mummies were split between two showcases, within the religion and sepulchral sections of the gallery. The 'sacred animals' case contained a wide variety of animal-form amulets, bronzes and some mummies 'to make the series of sacred animals more complete' (Gatty 1879, 13). The other case, 'animal mummies', contained the best examples from Mayer's collection, and a newly acquired ibis mummy from Saqqara 'attached to which is a human head with royal head-dress

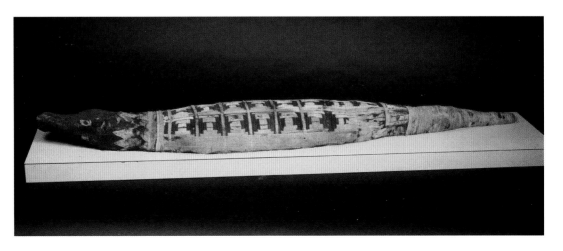

HORRIBLE RESULT OF USING THE "EGYPTIAN FUR-TILISER."

" A cargo of 180,000 mummified Cats has just been landed at Liverpool, to be used as Manure."—*Daily Paper*.

Fig. 45: Cartoon published in *Punch*, 15 February 1890.

Fig. 46: Cartoon of the second cat auction held at James Gordon and Co., Rumford Street, Liverpool, 10 February 1890. Published in *Daily Graphic*, 12 February 1890.

PUTTING MUMMY CATS UP TO AUCTION IN LIVERPOOL.

in cartonage [*sic*]' (Gatty 1879, 32). This object was sold to the museum on 20 September 1877 by the collector Rev. Greville Chester (1830–92), a regular visitor to the museum who each year sailed from Liverpool to spend the winter in Egypt. Since 1873 the Egyptologist Samuel Birch (1813–85) of the British Museum had been providing advice to Gatty about the collection. In 1877 he was asked by the museum's committee to write an assessment of the collection. Birch recommended selling items he considered to be unnecessary duplicates or inferior specimens. One year later three ibis mummies, four cat mummies and a cat's skull were just eight of the 636 items sold at Sotheby, Wilkinson and Hodge in London.

Twelve years later over 180,000 cat mummies arrived in Liverpool's port. During the nineteenth and twentieth centuries, most of the world's raw cotton came through Liverpool, on its way to Lancashire's textile mills. The city's banks financed the import of cotton from Egypt for Liverpool's cotton merchants, but in 1890 one bank, Kleinwort Sons & Co., was left with a shipment their client refused to accept. In the last week of January, SS *Pharos* sailed into the port carrying a cargo of nineteen and a half tons of unprocessed fertiliser – hundreds of bags of unwrapped mummified cats from near the village of Beni Hasan. The cats were auctioned at the knock down price of £3 13*s*. 9*d*. per ton to Leventon and Co., local fertilizer merchants who regularly shipped in animal bones from overseas, including Egypt. One of the partners provided the museum with a selection of the consignment and offered information of their discovery:

> *an Egyptian fellah digging in the sand near Beni-Hassan* [sic] *found his spade go through into a hole which on being opened out proved to be a large pit completely lined with these cats, each cat separately wrapped up in a kind of linen and other cloths. Many of the cats were wrapped in cloth of gaudy colours and richly embroidered material, others in plain linen. The people of the district collected and kept most of the cloth, and after a time the bones were collected, put into bags, and shipped to Liverpool.*

Leventon and Co. measured the levels of phosphate, lime and ammonia in the cats and offered the museum the results if it might give some guidance on their age and mummification technique. The museum put the cats on display, provided with a date of '2000 BC', and some were used to illustrate talks about the cargo at a meeting of the Biological Society by William Herdman, Professor of Natural History at the University of Liverpool, and Thomas Moore, the museum's Curator of Natural History. The story grew in the local news and on 10 February 1890, a second auction of eight and a half tons of cats from the same discovery, but from the SS *Thebes*' cargo, made the national news, with cartoons appearing in the *Daily Graphic* and *Punch* (Figs 45 and 46). As before, the auctioneer knocked the lot down using a cat's head for a gavel but this was more of a public spectacle; this time bone merchants were joined by an eager public now offered the opportunity of buying individual cat's heads, legs and paws – one partially wrapped cat's head and neck sold for four shillings. The publicity drove the price up and this time Leventon and Co. paid £5 7*s*. 6*d*. per ton, almost £2 more than the previous week.

More discoveries from Beni Hasan entered the museum following John Garstang's 1904–6 excavations of the lower cemetery below the terrace of rock-cut tombs (Garstang 1907a; Snape 2011, 160–3). Garstang's excavations were sponsored by a committee of patrons, who would often donate some of their share of the finds to the museum. In 1905 five members of the excavation committee donated finds from the first season of fieldwork at a cemetery on the west bank of the Nile, four kilometres to the northwest of Esna (see Garnett 3.5). A much needed extension had doubled the size of the museum and new galleries opened in 1906, with Egypt now the central feature in the spacious entrance hall; perhaps a reason the museum joined the excavation committee that year. The museum's division of finds included some mummified animals, including crocodile eggs wrapped in linen and plant fibre, although they do not appear on distribution lists. Garstang considered the 'graves of mummy birds and fish and crocodiles' to be a special feature contemporary with the Roman phase of the site, but acknowledges they were actually excavated by his team (Garstang 1907b, 142). The museum contributed £100 for a tenth of the finds, but the director disagreed with Garstang as he considered the museum's lot was unfair and contained 'objects too poor to exhibit' (Forbes 1907, 40, 52–4). The museum no longer subscribed to Garstang's excavations but continued to promote the university's fieldwork in the galleries.

Percy Newberry, Liverpool's first Professor of Egyptology, began cataloguing the collection in 1909 and designed a plan for a new display based on a typological basis that was only realised after World War I. The new arrangement did not leave much room for animal mummies – just one tall narrow showcase only suitable for upright displays of cats, ibises and hawks, with some room for a bundle of nine infant crocodiles and a tiny ram mummy. At the outbreak of World War II the museum moved some of the collection into newly reinforced basement storage and evacuated other items to bank vaults in the city, and stately homes in Cheshire and Wales. The largest objects were left in the gallery, including the collection of animal mummies and the museum remained open. On the night of 3 May 1941, a bomb weighing 225 kilograms fell on the library and the fire advanced into the adjoining Egyptian galleries (Allan 1941, 105–7). Whole showcases and sculptures were reduced to debris and just two animal mummies were salvaged. Those in storage fared better, especially Mayer's large crocodile mummy that escaped unharmed, but unfortunately only the charred bandaged head remains of Mayer's mummified adult dog. About 3000 Egyptian objects were either destroyed or beyond repair, and it would not be until 1976 that an Egyptian gallery reopened.

In the 40 years after the bombing, the collection increased in size with 10,000 new acquisitions coming from various sources around the country. By 1976, the number of animal mummies reached 67, the bulk coming from the collections of Norwich Castle Museum, who sold most of their foreign archaeology collections in 1956. In this group 12 collectors are represented and include familiar names in Egyptology, such as cat mummies from Robert Gayer-Anderson (1881–1945) and Greville Chester, but mainly donors from Norfolk, such as bird mummies from John Henry Gurney (1819–90), a leading ornithologist. Public appeals for donations were sometimes answered with a gift. One example was a cat mummy donated in 1950 by a resident of Colchester and collected by Sir Colin Scott-Moncrieff (1836–1916), a minister of public works during the British occupation of Egypt who held power within the antiquities service (Hollings 1917, 318–90). Larger collections also arrived, such as that of Josephine Gilstrap (1859–1943), a sponsor of Petrie's British School of Archaeology in Egypt, whose collection contained animal mummies from Kafr Ammar. Like many museums, Liverpool benefited from the dispersal of Sir Henry Wellcome's (1853–1936) vast collection of Egyptology. In 1971 it received 90 of the 300 crates dispersed to museums in the 1960s and 70s (Larson 2009, 275). The donation contained the skeleton of a bull from the Bucheum at Armant, and three animal mummies once collected by Rev. William MacGregor (1848–1937), a renowned collector from a wealthy Liverpool family who had sponsored Garstang's excavations.

The first animal mummies acquired after the Blitz also had a Liverpool connection as they were from Liverpool's Royal Institution on Colquitt Street, the same street as Mayer's Egyptian Museum. The Royal Institution was an educational establishment founded in 1814 and was open to everyone, with a small museum containing a good variety of Egyptian antiquities that Mayer would have seen when he first arrived in Liverpool. He may even have seen the fine cat mummy (Fig. 47) that came with the Royal Institution collection in 1942, donated to the museum before the war was even over. Such was the tenacity of Elaine Tankard (1901–69), curator of the collections between 1931 and 1966, who is responsible for much of what was rescued and replaced.

Fig. 47: Cat mummy donated by the Liverpool Royal Institution in 1942 and dated to the early Roman Period (Acc. No. 42.18.2, World Museum Liverpool). Reproduced by permission of National Museums Liverpool, World Museum.

3.8 Dealers, donors and doctors: exploring Glasgow's Egyptian collection

Gabrielle Heffernan and Brian Weightman

Museum collections reflect not only the objects themselves; they also provide a window on the men and women who donated their belongings, who developed the collections, and who worked with them.

Three accessioned objects currently in our collection provide an opportunity to examine some of the individuals, or groups, who shaped Glasgow Museum's Egyptian collection; John Galloway, the Misses Blackie, and Andrew T. Sandison, through whom various objects, including animal mummies, have entered into our care. Looking at their stories, we can understand more fully the ways in which collecting and care of objects has developed over the last 150 years. Much of the archival material relating to John Galloway and the Misses Blackie was recently collated and transcribed by a number of research volunteers, allowing a far greater understanding of the more recent history of these objects (Fig. 48).

The first, a mummified hawk (Acc. No. 1891.36.f), was donated to Glasgow Museums by John Galloway (Fig. 49). Born in Glasgow in 1830, he began work as a clerk at P. Henderson & Co. – a shipping firm – before rising to senior partner, then Director of the Irawaddy Flotilla Company and Chairman of the Glasgow Chamber of Commerce. Galloway donated 532 objects to Glasgow Museums between 1887 and 1903. The range of items provides an insight into his eclectic interests, covering everything from Scottish prehistoric archaeology and Peruvian ceramics to botanical and zoological specimens, as well as a number of Egyptian objects. As with many other prominent Glasgow businessmen, John Galloway seems to have acquired objects specifically for the purpose of enriching the museum collections.

Galloway's correspondence, held in the museum archives, demonstrates his commitment to this purpose. One letter (Acc. No. GMA.2014.3.8) dated 1892 attempted to persuade the committee in charge of museum finances to authorise a trip to Egypt by the curator, James Paton, to purchase antiquities. Galloway suggests 'five hundred pounds judiciously put out would give Glasgow an Egyptian Section in the Museum surpassed in Britain only by the British Museum' and, in addition, warns that prices were rising rapidly as 'natives and dealers … are discovering the worth of the articles they deal in'. Notes regarding the feasibility of the scheme were jotted down on the reverse of this letter, and so it would seem that Galloway's proposal was as least considered by the committee before being rejected. If his proposal had been accepted, Glasgow would indeed have been able to acquire a large number of objects, but whether this expenditure would have taken the collection to the status Galloway suggested, is more difficult to judge.

In addition to advice, Galloway also provided financial assistance. There are a number of letters from him (Acc. No. GMA.2014.3.3–4) in connection to his annual subscriptions to the Egypt Exploration Fund, which provided Glasgow Museums with a large proportion of its Egyptian collection. Unlike many other private collectors of this period, Galloway seems to have taken care to investigate and pass on to the museum as much information as possible regarding the provenance of his purchases.

In 1895, Galloway visited Dr Barnardo's Children's Home in Stepney Causeway, London, where, *in lieu* of a charitable donation, he purchased items from T. J. Woods' excavations at Ephesus which were being sold there to raise funds for the home. His letter asks the curator in Glasgow to instruct his staff 'that special care be taken of the little bits of paper containing description and authentication by Mrs Wood & that they are not parted from the articles to which they belong' (Acc. No. GMA.2014.3.2).

Another letter from 1903 concerning Egyptian antiquities relates how he had purchased items from the 'Gizah museum' and others from dealers but 'all had been authenticated by Brugsch' (Acc. No. GMA.2014.3.10). This indicates that Galloway acquired the material through consultation with the well-known Egyptologist and curator at the Bulaq Museum in Cairo, as did other collectors like Major William Joseph Myers, a contemporary traveller and enthusiast whose collection is now owned by Eton College. Myers' diaries also refer to many meetings with Emile Brugsch and purchases made on the recommendation of the museum official (Spurr 2000, 3).

However, John Galloway seems to have felt that he still retained some claim over his donated items even after they had entered Glasgow Museums' collection. A year after he had donated a human mummy and other

Fig. 48: A selection of the Museum's archive relating to the Egyptian collections © CSG CIC Glasgow Museums Collection.

Egyptian objects, he borrowed them to display at a lecture to the YMCA; although in deference to conservation issues, he did send for them in his 'best sprung cart' (Acc. No. GMA.2014.3.6).

The second object is a mummified cat (Acc. No. 29.b.1912) recorded as originating in the Ramesseum (Fig. 50), the memorial temple of Pharaoh Ramesses II, and donated by Marion and Clara Blackie in 1912. Initially exhibited during the same year in Glasgow's first exhibition of Egyptian objects, by 1914 this mummy was consigned to storage in the basement of Kelvingrove Art Gallery and Museum, seemingly due in some part at least to the attitudes of the museum authorities towards the donors themselves.

These two ladies were the daughters of Walter Graham Blackie, the famous Scottish publisher. Born into this wealthy family in 1852 and 1857, Marion and Clara had spent many years involved with charities for disadvantaged women in Glasgow. In 1932, Marion's work in this field was recognised by the award of an OBE.

The Blackies collected a limited number of antiquities, all of small size and easily portable. It seems likely, therefore, that their collection consisted of tourist souvenirs from a holiday in Egypt. By 1912, Marion and Clara were also involved with the women's emancipation movements and the peaceful Suffragist movement. It seems doubtful they would have approved of the more militant Suffragette attacks on objects in museums and galleries, including the Egyptian displays in the British Museum (Kavanagh 1994, 23). Other prominent Egyptologists, such as Amelia Edwards, founder of the Egypt Exploration Fund, Hilda Petrie and Margaret Murray, are all known to have connections to the emancipation movements, and many of the other contributors to Glasgow's first Egyptian exhibition also seem to have been sympathetic to this cause (Wilson 2013, personal communication).

In July 1912, Janet May Buchanan, a prominent figure in Scottish Egyptology, proposed mounting an exhibition of Egyptian objects in Kelvingrove. This was to consist of loans from

Fig. 49: Hawk mummy (Acc. No. 1891.367.f, Glasgow Museums) donated to Glasgow Museum by John Galloway © CSG CIC Glasgow Museums Collection.

her wide circle of friends who included professional Egyptologists such as W. M. Flinders Petrie (see Stevenson 3.2), as well as interested amateur collectors like the Blackies. With support from the then curator, James Paton, Buchanan herself curated the exhibition which opened in November that same year.

The accompanying catalogue to this exhibition contains a foreword by Petrie and an introductory section co-authored by Margaret Murray (Murray 1912, 20). In addition to the lists of articles loaned and their donors, this contains a section entitled the 'Position of Women' which stated that kingship in Egypt was inherited solely through the maternal line. In it, Murray applauded the status given to women in Egyptian society, comparing this favourably with other parts of the ancient world. In the context of the early twentieth-century campaign for suffrage, this may have been seen by some as overtly political; a view that possibly had an unforeseen effect on the Blackies' and other collections in the years to follow.

Buchanan was tragically killed in December 1912 and a memorial fund was set up in her name to purchase Egyptian objects for Glasgow Museums. Administered by the Glasgow branch of the Egyptian Research Students Association (ERSA), this raised large sums of money in a short space of time, which enabled the purchase of several hundred artefacts as well as donations of objects such as the Blackies' mummified cat. This important collection was then passed into the care of Glasgow Museums where

unfortunately at that time it was not given the attention it deserved (Eccles 2012, personal communication).

Two years after the first Egyptian exhibition, a new catalogue was produced by the Rev. Colin Campbell with an introduction by the curator, James Paton (Campbell 1914). In this catalogue, items donated by Galloway, the Egypt Exploration Fund and other male donors (including Campbell himself) are listed and described. However, all the objects from the J. May Buchanan Memorial Collection, including those from Petrie's BSAE excavations, were not displayed or mentioned. All of these objects had been consigned to the publicly inaccessible museum stores.

This deliberate removal of all public traces of the previous exhibition, and all donations associated with it, is difficult to explain aesthetically or academically. There were many archaeologically important objects within this group, and so the suspicion arises that this decision was based on personal prejudice against the political views of the donors. This was highlighted by Margaret Murray's exhibition introduction two years earlier and the work of the Blackie sisters, among others, in the fight for female emancipation.

In some cases, this attitude and the lack of interest shown in the donations to the museum has caused confusion in the records. This becomes problematic to rectify today with, for example, objects from the Buchanan collection having become disassociated from their correct accession numbers and recorded locations. In other cases, objects were never re-displayed after their removal in 1914, as was the case with our mummified cat. However, by careful study of the archival material it is becoming possible to re-discover more details of the important role played by Janet May Buchanan, Marion and Clara Blackie and the other members of Glasgow's ERSA in the growth of Glasgow Museums' Egyptian collection.

Further examination of Glasgow Museums' collections uncovered a small mummified falcon (Acc. No. A.2007.1.12) which dates to the Late-Roman Periods (Fig. 51). This example is one of several that originate from the collection of our third donor, Andrew T. Sandison.

Sandison was better known as a pathologist, holding a research position at the University of Glasgow from 1948. It was through his scientific research that he became acquainted with the ancient world, and in particular that of the Egyptians, as he became increasingly fascinated by ancient pathology and disease. His edited volume, *Disease in Antiquity*, which he co-authored with the bioarchaeologist Don Brothwell (see Brothwell foreword), pays tribute to his considerable interest in the subject.

As his reputation as a scholar of ancient remains grew, his expertise was sought by members of the Egyptology community. One of these was Cyril Aldred, who co-authored an article with Sandison (Aldred and Sandison 1961), which examined depictions of the eighteenth Dynasty pharaoh, Akhenaten. They concluded that not only did he likely suffer from endocrine disease, but also that the much debated mummy in the Theban royal tomb, KV55, is likely to be that of the same king. Such research drew together Sandison's existing knowledge of the human body with his growing understanding of Egyptian history and culture.

From this grew Sandison's interest in Egyptian mummification. In 1961 he acquired several human and animal remains for his laboratory at Glasgow's Western Infirmary, to allow him to continue his research into the topic. While many of these remains were Egyptian, some were from others countries such as Chile.

Studying mummified remains allowed him to increase his knowledge of the practice, but it was only through experimental studies that a full understanding could be gained. To this end he began work to recreate the process of mummification in his own laboratory. He used modern human specimens, usually fingers or toes, and carried out varying procedures to mummify them in an attempt to identify the most effective one. He published some of his findings in the *Journal of Near Eastern Studies*, in an article that examines the correct usage of the

Fig. 50: Cat mummy (Acc. No. 29.b.1912, Glasgow Museums) donated by Marion and Clara Blackie in 1912 © CSG CIC Glasgow Museums Collection.

Fig. 51: Falcon
mummy (Acc. No.
A.2007.1.12, Glasgow
Museums) donated by
Andrew T. Sandison
© CSG CIC Glasgow
Museums Collection.

mineral natron in the embalming process, and concluding, in this instance, that it was probably used in a solid form by the ancient Egyptians (Sandison 1963).

The animal mummies in Sandison's collections form part of his investigations into the peculiarities of mummification. Their value for his studies in human pathology is, undeniably, negligible, but as examples of mummification they are invaluable. Through, for example, the unwrapped cat's head now in Glasgow's collection (Acc. No. A.2007.1.10), Sandison would have been able to study the treatment of the body and the way in which wrappings were applied, while the falcon, already mentioned, demonstrated the finished product.

Sandison died in 1982 having published only a small amount of his research into

mummification, and his collection was deposited with Glasgow Museums. Sandison did not only appreciate these objects as representatives of a distant culture, he saw them as an opportunity to connect modern scientific understanding with the forgotten science of the past. He didn't simply ask *what?* or *why?* but also *how?*

Each of these stories helps us to understand a little more about how Glasgow Museums' collection came to be, and how it has been developed through the years. While Galloway's dedication helped to shape the early collection, the work of the Misses Blackie, and others with them, focused on its development and display, albeit limited by the society in which they lived. Finally, the work of Sandison posed scientific questions, pulling the collection, and our perception of it, into a new era of understanding.

3.9 The mummies of Cottonopolis: the Manchester Museum collection

Campbell Price

Manchester Museum opened in 1890 in a purpose-built building designed by the architect Alfred Waterhouse, holding collections used to support the teaching of the natural sciences in the Victoria University of Manchester. Much of the material derived from the Manchester Natural History Society and was curated by the Museum's first Keeper, the geologist and prehistorian, William Boyd Dawkins (1837–1929). Over time the Museum acquired and displayed natural history specimens and objects from human cultures, including Egyptology (Alberti 2009).

The core of Manchester's Egyptian and Sudanese collection was formed in large part through the generosity of one man: Jesse Haworth (1835–1920), a wealthy Mancunian cotton trader at a time when Manchester had become known as 'Cottonopolis' (Fig. 52) Haworth is said to have been inspired by reading Amelia Edwards' travelogue *A Thousand Miles Up The Nile* (1877), and was encouraged by Miss Edwards to support Flinders Petrie's work in Egypt. Along with H. Martyn Kennard, Haworth was Petrie's main financial backer between 1888 and 1892, and continued to support the British School of Archaeology in Egypt and Egypt Exploration Society thereafter (David 1986, 4–7). The generosity of Haworth enabled several extensions to the Museum, including a new building dedicated to Egyptology opened in October 1912. The Manchester Museum Egyptology collections are now amongst the largest in Britain, numbering around 18,000 objects, and include some forty-six animal mummies.

Funded excavations

Despite the Museum's strong support for archaeological work in Egypt, most of the examples of animal mummies in the collection lack a firm provenance. Those that derive from controlled excavations can be traced to a small number of known sources. Unsurprisingly, the Manchester collection contains several crocodile mummies from Petrie's Haworth-funded excavations at Hawara (1888–9). Petrie remarked on the great quantities of crocodile mummies all over the site. While some were apparently buried in reused non-royal tombs, others were found in less discrete groups amidst the limestone chips of earlier buildings. Petrie (1889, 10) observed that the large number of mummies related to their ancient function:

> In every direction the work brought up crocodiles, of all sizes, from monsters 15 feet long, to infants, and even eggs. The apparent number was swelled moreover by quantities of dummies, evidently made for a ceremonial purpose. The imitation crocodile mummies consist of bundles of reeds or grass, with an egg or only a single bone inside; and they seem to have been intended to testify a worshipper's devotion to Sebek [sic] by such pious care bestowed on the sacred animal: doubtless their preparation and sale was a priestly trade.

Examples with firm provenance include the mummy of a mammal, possibly a puppy, from Gurob (Acc. No. 563) and an ibis bird from Abydos (Acc. No. 6098) (McKnight 2010, 128–9). In 1920, the mummy of a cat was purchased from the excavator John Garstang (see Garnett 3.5). Three much less attractive cats with a putative Beni Hasan provenance are more likely to have come from large shipments of the animals to Liverpool (Fig. 53) (see Cooke 3.7).

The final years of the archaeological finds

Fig. 52: Jesse Haworth (1835–1920), in the doctoral robes of The University of Manchester, having been honoured for his beneficence to the University. Reproduced by permission of Manchester Museum, The University of Manchester.

Fig. 53: Head of a cat mummy (Acc. No. 12015, Manchester Museum) from Beni Hasan. Photo: Alan Seabright. Reproduced by permission of Manchester Museum, The University of Manchester.

division system in Egypt ended in 1983 and are represented by, amongst others, an ibis mummy from the Egypt Exploration Society excavations at Saqqara (Acc. No. 11501) (see Nicholson 3.4). This example shows the characteristic appliqué design (cf. Figs 21 and 100) recorded in other examples from the site (Emery 1965a, pl. 5).

Private collections

Saqqara may be the source of a number of other animal mummies in the collection, although identification is reliant on archival information. Thomas Alfred Coward (1867–1933), an ornithologist and Acting Keeper of Manchester Museum during the First World War, donated an impressive wooden cat coffin (Acc. No. 9303a-b) with its occupant still intact (Fig. 54). A letter survives from Coward, dated 27 October 1921, to the excavator James Quibell. In it, Coward expresses delight at the quality of the specimen and jokes that the Assistant Keeper in charge of archaeology, Winifred Crompton, had a particular liking for the piece:

> *The long expected lot has arrived. It is a beauty, and I want to thank you very much for selecting it. I had not seen one in a case before. The one by post, of course, came long ago, but this one seems to have taken its time!*
>
> *As I believe you got it from a dealer, you may have no idea where it was found, but can you give me any approximate period or date for it? I had to see Miss Crompton put it in a Tac case, or I think she would have taken it home to see if she could make it purr.*

A brief note pencilled by Quibell in reply on the reverse of the same letter affirms that the cat coffin in fact came from the excavations conducted by Cecil Firth at Saqqara. By chance, a surviving photograph of uncertain date shows Firth at Saqqara surrounded by artistically arranged bronze cats and cat coffins (Fig. 55). This includes in the foreground a coffin which in all probability is the Manchester example, thereby confirming its provenance. Coward's interest in the piece is likely to have been zoological, so it is remarkable that the coffin remained intact.

No fewer than half a dozen animal mummies were donated to the Museum by the family of a prolific collector, Max Emil Robinow (1845–1900) (Fig. 56). Robinow was a German émigré born in Hamburg, who made money in the shipping industry based in Manchester and took up British citizenship in 1875 (Price and Scott forthcoming). He travelled to Egypt at least once, in the winter of 1895–6, and competed with other collectors to acquire antiquities. Robinow became friends with Jesse Haworth and through him with Flinders Petrie, from whom it is likely that he acquired part of his collection. Although Robinow seems to have

Fig. 54: Cat coffin from
Saqqara (Acc. No. 9303a-b,
Manchester Museum)
containing a mummified
cat. Photo: Alan Seabright.
Reproduced by permission
of Manchester Museum,
The University of
Manchester.

Fig. 55: Cecil Firth at Saqqara, surrounded by cat coffins and bronze figurines, date unknown. Photograph © 2015 Museum of Fine Arts, Boston.

Fig. 56: Max Emil Robinow (1845–1900), the donor of a major collection of objects to the Museum. Reproduced by kind permission of John Booth.

collected pieces based on aesthetic quality, his interest in Egyptian culture extended to animal, as well as human, mummies.

In keeping with many other museums, several animal mummies came into the Manchester collection from donors about which little or nothing is known. Some of these are likely to have been donated because of Manchester Museum's reputation as a centre for the study of mummified remains from ancient Egypt.

In 1908, Manchester hosted the public unwrapping of two human mummies discovered by one of Petrie's apprentices at Deir Rifeh in Middle Egypt. The unwrapping was conducted by Margaret Murray and a group of other specialists in different fields assembled for the purpose. In 1975, Rosalie David, the curator in charge of Egyptology at the Museum, launched the Manchester Museum Mummy Project, which used a range of techniques to investigate Egyptian mummies – including those of animals (David 1979, 13–15) (see David Foreword) (Fig. 57). This set in motion developments in analytical techniques that confirmed Manchester's place at the forefront of mummy studies, and led to the establishment of the Ancient Egyptian Animal Bio Bank.

Fig. 57: The Egyptology galleries in the 1960s, showing human and animal mummies displayed together. Reproduced by permission of Manchester Museum, The University of Manchester.

4   Animal Mummy Investigations at Manchester

…it has long been recognised that a more modern multi-disciplinary treatment is required, giving not only the result of analyses and techno-logical investigations but also explicitly stating the means by which they were obtained.
(Nicholson and Shaw 2000, 1)

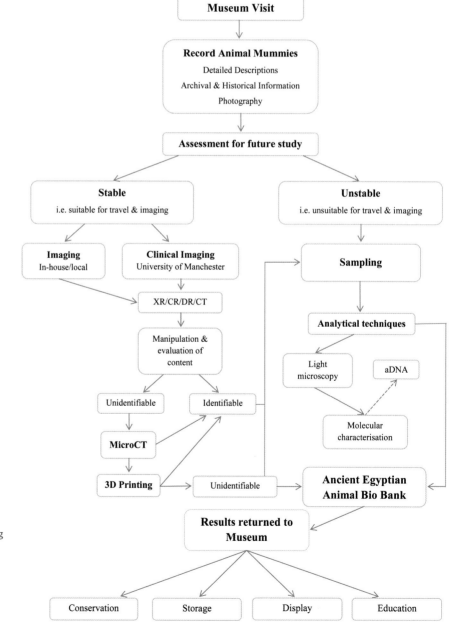

Fig. 58: Diagram showing the protocol followed at Manchester for the study of mummified animals. Reproduced courtesy of Stephanie Atherton-Woolham.

4.1 The Ancient Egyptian Animal Bio Bank

Lidija McKnight

Animal mummy research has always been some way behind that of human mummies; however, projects seeking to redress this balance are now underway. In 1999, when studying Archaeology at the University of York, the author embarked on a research project to study animal mummies from the Bolton Library and Museums Services (McKnight 2010; McKnight [née Owen] 2001). Plain film radiography was conducted using a portable unit, with the images hand-developed in a tiny broom-cupboard. Since such humble beginnings, the quest to understand animal mummification continued at The University of Manchester, investigating British collections using non-invasive imaging techniques.

In June 2010, the Ancient Egyptian Animal Bio Bank was established as a formal continuation of this research, incorporating a multi-disciplinary team (McKnight et al. 2011). The initial aim was to collate information relating to mummified animal remains in museum collections outside Egypt, beginning with those in Britain. This was an ambitious target as the material was widely distributed in museums, galleries, societies, schools and private collections. A pilot study of northern British museums resulted in the visual (macroscopic)

and radiographic study of 177 animal mummies, which formed the original Bio Bank entries (McKnight *et al.* in press b).

At the time of writing in late 2014, the Bio Bank includes 797 mummies from 52 British collections, alongside three major international collections: the Museum of Fine Arts, Boston and the Oriental Institute, Chicago in the USA and Musei Vaticani, Vatican City. Research is led by two associates, alongside several advisors and experts in their respective fields; many of whom have contributed to this book. This combination has enabled questions regarding the nature and purpose of animal mummification to be approached in the most comprehensive manner, thus optimising the validity of archaeological and scientific inquiry.

Scientific research, including that conducted on animal mummies, should follow a logical and ethical process, with techniques employed according to the suitability of the mummy or associated samples to answer specific research questions (Fig. 58). This chapter describes this process, phase-by-phase, to explain the questions asked of the material and the variety of techniques that can be applied to answer them.

In the Museum Setting

4.2 Archival and historical investigation

Lidija McKnight and Stephanie Atherton-Woolham

Before visiting a museum with animal mummies, information relating to the size of the collection is obtained which enables logistical planning. In addition, specific acquisition details and provenance (geographical and chronological) are obtained where available; however, this is generally rare for animal mummies. Over the course of their curation (often over two centuries and between several owners), it is not surprising that this information has gone astray. Details about the excavators, donors and collectors associated with the material can provide context for individual artefacts (see 3 – Egypt and the British: Archaeologists, Collectors and Collections).

Documentation of previous research is vital to avoid unnecessary duplication of analysis. Where previous radiographs exist, a report is compiled for posterity and image quality is assessed to evaluate whether repeat investigation is necessary. As a rule, radiographs acquired over ten years ago merit repeat analysis using modern radiographic equipment.

Fig. 59: Photographing animal mummies. Photo: Alan Seabright. Reproduced by permission of Manchester Museum, The University of Manchester.

4.3 A picture tells a thousand words: visual inspection and photography of animal mummies

Lidija McKnight

Simple macroscopic assessment is important as the initial research technique. Dimensions (in millimetres), shape and decorative style are recorded, alongside their placement within a chronological and geographical typology (Atherton 2012). Mummy bundles are classified as 'plain' or 'stylised' depending on the level of decoration, with their shape categorised as 'wrapped to shape of contents', 'conical', 'skittle', 'amorphous' or 'modelled'. Bundle form often indicates that a certain species is contained within. In particular, ibises are often contained within conical bundles, whereas cat mummies tend to be 'skittle' shaped (Zivie and Lichtenberg 2005, 116–17), often with modelled facial features (McKnight 2015).

Photography captures the visual appearance of a mummified bundle and creates a snapshot of an artefact at a clearly defined moment in time. This is important for all objects in museum collections, which may be affected by the conditions in which they are stored or displayed, in addition to the effects of time. Anomalies, changes to appearance and preservation can be revealed by comparing photographs acquired at different times. This often highlights episodes of human intervention, alongside environmental and accidental damage.

A digital SLR camera and plain backdrop are used to acquire images from every available projection, allowing a comprehensive record of the mummy bundle to be made (Fig. 59). Mummies are, by their very nature, fragile, and care must be taken at all times during investigation to ensure that they are handled only when necessary and under the guidance of museum staff (Fig. 60).

Digital image capture methods, whether photographic or radiographic, offer not only the ability for swift recording, but also ease of dissemination between museums and researchers. This is of particular use for improved museum interpretation; images offer greater understanding of the mummy bundles and their contents, improving engagement between the visitor and the artefact.

Fig. 60: Positioning mummies for study. Photo: Alan Seabright. Reproduced by permission of Manchester Museum, The University of Manchester.

In the Clinical Setting

4.4 Imaging animal mummies: history and techniques

Judith Adams

The practice of human and animal mummification has resulted in a large number of items being available for research today. Such artefacts can provide valuable insights into the way of life, the health of the population and the rituals exercised in ancient Egypt. During the nineteenth and early twentieth centuries, 'mummy unrollings', whereby mummies were unwrapped and dissected, were widely practised, yet with little documentation of the findings (Moshenska 2014) (see McKnight and Price 3.1). This destructive practice, which resulted in the loss of a valuable scientific resource, has been replaced by imaging. Its impact in the non-destructive study of mummified remains is great, enabling a 'peep inside' a mummy to reveal its secrets.

Wilhelm Roentgen discovered X-rays in December 1895 (Boni et al. 2004) and four months later a mummified child and a cat from the Senckenberg Museum in Frankfurt, Germany, were studied in this way (Koenig 1896). Thurston Holland radiographed a mummified bird from the Liverpool Museum during the same year (Holland 1937). Although the effects of radiation exposure on the living were not yet fully understood, mummies represented excellent candidates upon which to test the technique, having died many centuries before. Imaging has become more widely exploited since that time and was applied to the study of human, rather than animal, mummies. Such studies included those by Flinders Petrie (1898), and Sir Grafton Elliot Smith and Howard Carter (Smith 1912). In 1931, Moodie surveyed mummies in the Chicago Field Museum (Moodie 1931) and in 1960 Gray documented the radiographic findings of 193 mummies from museums in Europe and Britain (Adams and Alsop 2008; Dawson and Gray 1968; Gray 1966; 1973; Gray and Slow 1968).

Computed tomography (CT) was introduced in 1972, initially to image the human brain transforming the practice of neuroradiology (Hounsfield 1973). Subsequently, from 1975 whole body CT scanners were available. This imaging technique had a huge impact on clinical diagnosis and management in patients, and is extensively used for these purposes. Having first been applied in 1979 to the study of mummies in Canada (Harwood-Nash 1979) and in Manchester (Isherwood *et al.* 1979), CT has become the most widely used imaging method. Biomedical research in the study of Egyptian artefacts, including imaging, began in the 1970s at The University of Manchester, established by Professor Rosalie David and colleagues at the KNH Centre for Biomedical Egyptology (David 1979).

Mummified animal remains from Egypt are much less extensively studied than human mummies, although The University of Manchester studied approximately 280 animal mummies between 2000 and 2012 using imaging (McKnight 2010; McKnight *et al.* 2011; McKnight *et al.* in press b). All were imaged out-of-hours in the radiology departments in the Central Manchester University Hospital NHS Foundation Trust and the sessions never interfered with clinical imaging of patients. Initially, imaging took place in the adult department of the Manchester Royal Infirmary where there are two CT scanners. However, with the increasing clinical demand for CT in adults, extended working hours from 8am to 8pm had to be introduced. Additionally, heavy emergency use outside these hours made access for imaging of mummies problematic. Consequently, imaging of mummies has moved to the Royal Manchester Children's Hospital. The use of CT in children's medicine is less frequent due to the application of the ALARA principle (As Low As Reasonably Achievable), which determines acceptable levels of ionizing radiation exposure. As CT involves significant doses, it is used much less frequently in children, making access more feasible.

Imaging techniques

Both radiographs and CT use the interaction of X-rays with tissues and structures of different density (determined by atomic number and proton density). In dense tissue, such as bone and metal, most X-rays are absorbed and do not reach the medium (radiographic film, photosensitive cassettes or sensitive detectors), which record the X-ray photons that pass through the item being imaged. These structures appear white in images. In areas of low density material, such as air or fat, most X-ray photons pass through to reach the recording medium and will appear black. Structures of intermediate density will be varying shades of grey between these two extremes.

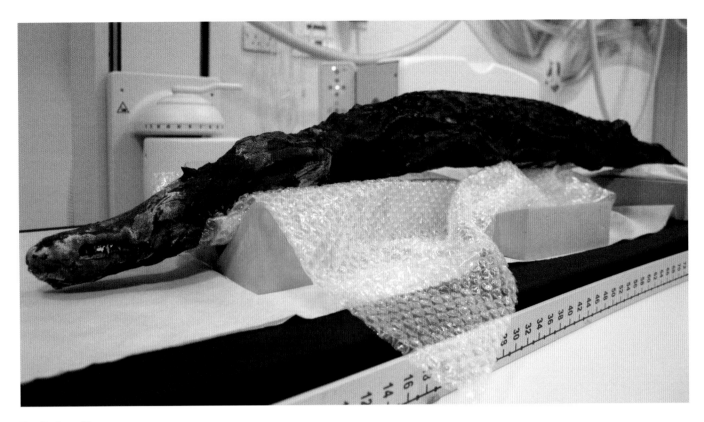

Fig. 61: Crocodile mummy (Acc. No. 1772, Manchester Museum) on the X-ray table supported by foam blocks. Photo: Lidija McKnight.

Radiographs

In early mummy studies, radiographs were performed with portable X-ray equipment in museums or in the field. However, image quality was limited, which would be improved if acquired using equipment housed in hospital departments, where such imaging is now generally performed. Images were initially captured on hard copy silver-coated film, of which there would be only a single copy. Radiography was repeated if the image was under-or over-exposed. However, with the introduction of Picture Archiving and Communication Systems (PACS) in the early 2000s, the image is now captured electronically in digital format. Initially this was with computed radiography (CR) in which the imaging plate is housed in a cassette, similar to traditional film/screen X-ray systems. More recently digital radiography (DR) is increasingly used in which the image is captured directly onto a sensitive flat panel detector without a cassette. DR therefore acquires the image more rapidly, utilizes lower doses of ionizing radiation and has higher spatial resolution (influencing the visualisation of small objects) than CR. Digital images have the advantage of being able to be manipulated and viewed at multiple sites and on various devices with appropriate software (e.g. OsirixTM, Pixmeo, Switzerland), but have lower spatial resolution (0.25 mm in DR) than hard copy film (0.1 mm).

Radiographs, however acquired, have the advantage of being widely available and inexpensive. However, a limitation of radiographs is that they are two-dimensional images of three-dimensional objects, which causes superimposition of structures resulting in problems with identification. To counteract this, two views are generally produced at right angles (anterior posterior and lateral).

Many groups no longer perform radiographs, but the 'quick look' at what mummy bundles contain, and the superior spatial resolution (0.25) over CT (0.6 mm), means that they are considered essential in mummy studies at Manchester.

Computed tomography (CT)

When CT technology was first introduced in 1972, a pencil beam of X-rays rotated around a patient and the emerging beam was measured by a detector. Later, a fan beam of X-rays and an arc of detectors were used, and by rotating around the patient, many hundreds of transmitted radiation readings were obtained. With powerful computing these are displayed as transverse axial slices through the body; initially as individual sections 5–10 mm in thickness. Each slice is made up of individual picture elements (voxels) which are given a value depending on the X-ray attenuation of the contents (in Hounsfield units; HU). This

Fig. 62: Photograph, radiograph and coronal reformat of shrew mummy (Acc. No. 6033, Manchester Museum). Photo: Alan Seabright. Reproduced by permission of Manchester Museum, Lidija McKnight and the Ancient Egyptian Animal Bio Bank, The University of Manchester.

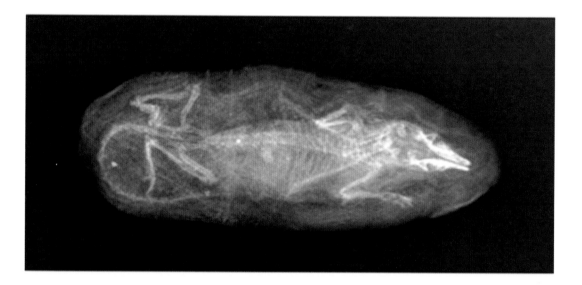

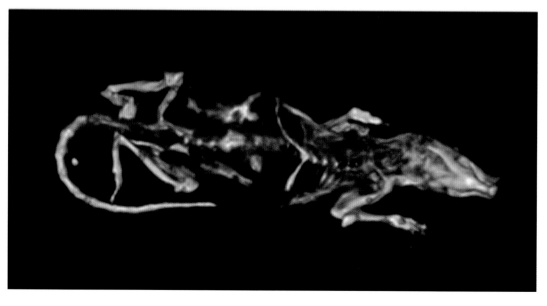

enables quantitative measurement of the voxel contents.

Over the past two decades great technological developments have occurred in CT, which include a rotating X-ray tube and rings of detectors (initially 4, then 16, 32, 64, 128 and a maximum of 256) (multi-detector spiral CT; MDCT). The patient lies on a table which moves through the gantry. This enables rapid acquisition of images,[*] with improved spatial resolution (generally 0.6 mm); the ability to manipulate the data to reconstruct images in the coronal or sagittal planes; and 3D volumetric images with surface rendering, depending on what structures are to be depicted. Using the latter, the mummy bundle can be virtually 'unwrapped' to display its contents. Recently dual energy CT using two X-ray tubes positioned at 90° angles to one another, running either at the same energy (kV, enabling even more rapid image acquisition) or at two different energies[†] has been employed on mummified material (Taylor and Antoine 2014, 20).

The strengths of CT are rapid acquisition of images, quantitation (measurement of density and size) and 3D manipulation of data. However, the technique is expensive, sometimes difficult to access, and the large amount of data acquired takes up considerable space in PACS.

Practical considerations

Mummies are inflexible artefacts and often require positioning with foam supports to achieve optimum images (Fig. 61). They are frequently imaged within their protective packaging both to expedite the process, to minimize handling and protect the artefacts from unnecessary damage. So that images can be found easily in PACS, and in order that radiographs and CT images are stored in the same digital 'package', it is essential that mummies are booked in as patients before the start of the imaging session. We use the surname 'Mummy', and the unique Bio Bank number and brief description of the item e.g. 'AEABB123 cat', as the first name. Also invaluable is a team of experienced radiographers who are enthusiastic and willing to work outside normal working hours.

Other clinical imaging techniques

Ultrasound scanning (US) and magnetic resonance imaging (MRI) are important and widely used imaging techniques in clinical medicine. However, both depend on the presence of water within the body and so are not applicable to mummified tissues, which are preserved through desiccation. These techniques are infrequently performed as the rehydration of desiccated tissue, ultimately a destructive technique, is not ethical.

Application of imaging to animal mummies

The team use both radiographs (CR and DR) and MDCT with reformations on all the animal mummies studied at The University of Manchester (Fig. 62). Insurance and transportation of the valuable items from museums, their safe keeping and careful handling during imaging, are ensured by having appropriate, experienced personnel present so that radiologists/radiographers can concentrate on optimising image quality.

There are some specific challenges in imaging animal mummy bundles, which are often small in size. Clinical body scanners, designed for human patients, use limited doses of ionizing radiation and are restricted by their large gantry (ring) size, both of which affect spatial resolution when imaging small objects. CT of animal mummies measuring less than 5 cm² produces images of limited definition.

When imaging the structure of trabecular and cortical bone in peripheral skeletal sites (hands and feet) in humans, high resolution CT (HRpCT) offers a spatial resolution of 130 μm. This standard setting has proved optimal for imaging animal mummies.

Micro-CT scanners are available to scan small objects *in-vivo* or *in-vitro* with much higher spatial resolutions of between 10–60 μm. These offer advantages in the imaging of small animal mummies in which movement is not a problem (exposure times in such scanners are often long) (see McKnight and Bibb 4.6).

Conclusions

Imaging has played an important role in the study of human mummies over many years, but scientific studies in animal mummies are more disparate. Imaging, both radiographs and MDCT, has much to offer in the study of animal mummies, in particular the contents of the mummy bundle, and the ability to provide insight into the life and traditions of ancient Egypt.

---

[*] In original scanners each 2D section took 20 seconds to acquire; now the entire torso is acquired in this time.

[†] This enhances visualisation and quantitation of high density structures, such as calcium and bone.

4.5 What lies beneath: imaging animal mummies

Lidija McKnight

Radiographic imaging is routinely used in the clinical setting to diagnose trauma and in the identification and evaluation of disease. Successfully applied to mummified material, it enables a non-invasive insight into the contents of wrapped mummy bundles.

True and pseudo animal mummies

We often expect an animal mummy to contain a single, complete body represented by the external appearance taking on a certain form, or through decorative details, which give a more lifelike representation. However, quantitative research has demonstrated that this is only true for around half of the mummy bundles studied (Fig. 63).

The presence of isolated and fragmented bone from a variety of animals (and sometimes humans), in addition to material such as feather, eggshell, plant material and linen, have been noted (Kessler and Nur el-Din 2005, 159; McKnight 2010; McKnight *et al.* 2015).

The presence of alternatives to a single complete animal has previously been interpreted as evidence of the struggle to meet the high demand for votive offerings. Literary evidence from Saqqara, particularly the *Archive of Hor*, and archaeological observations of the mummy bundles, which record the dedication of fragmentary bones and empty bundles, have added weight to this theory (Ray 1976, 142–3). Such mummies were recorded as 'fakes' or 'pseudos' (for example Ikram 2005, 14); however, research at The University of Manchester supports theories that the word 'fake' is misleading (Bruno 2013, 121–3; McKnight and Atherton 2014, 109). Radiography shows that around a quarter of the mummies contain the fragmentary remains of either less or more than one individual, sometimes from multiple species (Fig. 64). These bundles, irrespective of the amount of skeletal material contained within, are termed 'true' mummies (McKnight and Atherton 2014).

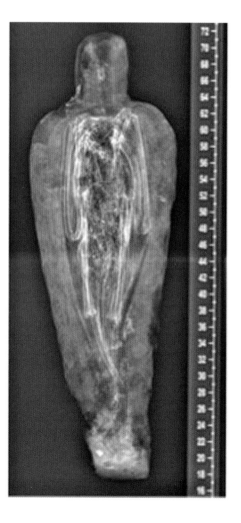

Fig. 63: Photograph and radiograph of an ibis mummy (Acc. No. 6098, Manchester Museum) showing a single complete, articulated skeleton. Reproduced by permission of Manchester Museum, Lidija McKnight and the Ancient Egyptian Animal Bio Bank, The University of Manchester.

Fig. 64: Hawk mummy
(Acc. No. 4295, Manchester
Museum) showing
incomplete, disarticulated
bird remains (top) and
fish mummy (Acc. No.
1.1983.?, Bolton Library
and Museums Services)
showing the presence of
two individuals (bottom).
Reproduced by permission
of Manchester Museum,
Lidija McKnight and the
Ancient Egyptian Animal
Bio Bank, The University of
Manchester.

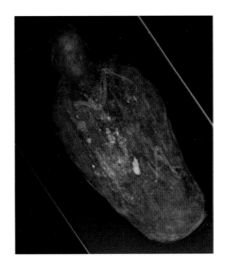
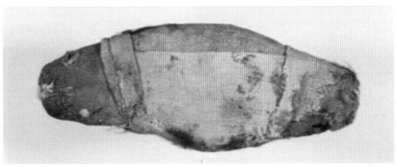

Fig. 65: Pseudo mummy
(Acc. No. UC.30693, Petrie
Museum of Egyptian
Archaeology) containing
the remains of three bird
eggs. Scan performed
by Robert Hill at the
Portland Hospital, London
Photo and reformat: Lidija
McKnight. Reproduced by
permission of the Ancient
Egyptian Animal Bio
Bank, The University of
Manchester.

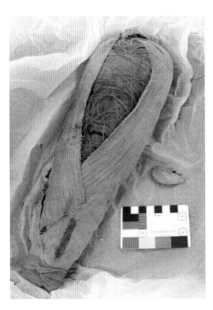
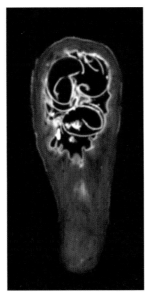

The remaining quarter contain no skeletal material and are termed 'pseudo' mummies (Fig. 65). They likely result from the collection of materials deemed to have sacred associations, either because of their proximity to the living animals or their placement within a sacred landscape.[*] Both animate and inanimate objects within a sacred landscape were therefore afforded ritual significance (see Atherton-Woolham and McKnight 2.2).

---

[*]   This has parallels with the careful preservation of
    human embalming detritus (Eaton-Krauss 2008).

 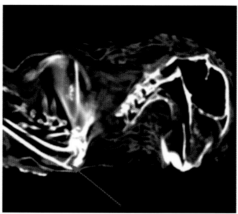

Fig. 66: Cat mummy (Acc. No. DBYMU1929-189/1, Derby Museum) and sagittal reformat with arrow marking a partially fused epiphysis on the proximal humerus. Photo and reformat: Lidija McKnight. Reproduced by permission of the Ancient Egyptian Animal Bio Bank, The University of Manchester.

Ageing

Bundle size can be used as a rough indicator of age; however, this only stands true when a complete skeleton is present. Bundles which resemble an animal, but which appear comparatively small, are often found to contain either incomplete skeletal remains or non-skeletal material.

Zooarchaeologists determine age by examining the eruption of the dentition (the stage of dental development) and the stage of epiphyseal fusion (predetermined age markers at which specific skeletal elements fuse) (Fig. 66). With wrapped mummy bundles, several factors affect whether such analysis can be conducted, including the state of preservation, which skeletal elements are present, and whether radiography enables their clear visualisation.

Cause of death and pathology

Natural curiosity leads us to question how things died. Previous human and animal mummy research endeavoured to identify pathology, including trauma, disease and cause of death (Armitage and Clutton-Brock 1981; Adams 1864; Ikram 2005; Zivie and Lichtenberg 2005). Modern diagnostic radiography enables pathology in living patients to be easily identified; however, taphonomic changes caused by mummification and the burial environment can alter tissue composition in mummified bodies, which makes identification of these markers problematic. Occasionally, pathology was noted in preserved human remains (Aufderheide 2003, 382–5; 418–63); however, small animal mummy bundles with highly compressed wrappings can complicate visualisation.

Interpretation of previous studies on votive cat mummies suggested that animals were intentionally slaughtered by trauma to the cervical spine, indicating death by asphyxiation (Armitage and Clutton-Brock 1981, 195);

however, only seven of the 53 cats studied showed displaced fractures of this nature. The identification of fatal pathologies in mummified votive remains is difficult to isolate from post-mortem 'pseudo-pathologies', caused by mummification and the fragility of the desiccated remains (Fig. 67) (Atherton-Woolham and McKnight 2014). Of the mummies studied to date in Manchester, only one specimen (Acc. No. 1772) demonstrated fatal pathology, in the form of a depressed fracture to the skull vault, indicative of blunt force trauma (Fig. 68).

Animals used as votive offerings demonstrated minimal ante-mortem pathology. Estimates at Tuna el-Gebel indicated that only 0.5% of bird remains studied showed pathological markers (Von den Driesch et al. 2006, 226). Manchester research revealed a single example; a healed fracture in the femur of a Sacred Ibis (Atherton et al. 2012). Low frequencies of pathology, caused by disease rather than through trauma, are attributed to the relatively short lifespans of these animals, during which time pathologies were generally incapable of affecting the skeleton (Adams and Alsop 2008, 36–7). Furthermore, temple staff officiating in the cult may have preferentially culled animals presenting signs of trauma or disease, thereby reducing the risk to other animals and ensuring adequate provision for the healthy population.

Evidence suggesting that farmed animal populations supplied the demand for the votive industry is thought to manifest itself in disease and inadequate nutrition (Armitage and Clutton-Brock 1981, 194–5; Ikram 2005, 12). Harris Lines, caused by the cessation of bone ossification during periods of stress, malnutrition and illness (Adams and Alsop 2005, 36; Harris 1933, 87), were identified in animal mummies. However, their frequent occurrence in wild and captive animals, as demonstrated by modern veterinary studies, indicates that they

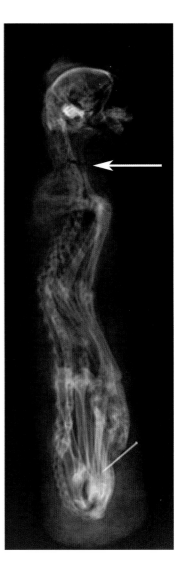

Fig. 67: Cat mummy (Acc. No. Ha6356, Bristol City Museum and Art Gallery) and lateral radiograph showing a post-mummification fracture through the cervical spine and extensive damage to the skull. Photo: Lidija McKnight. Reproduced by permission of the Ancient Egyptian Animal Bio Bank, The University of Manchester.

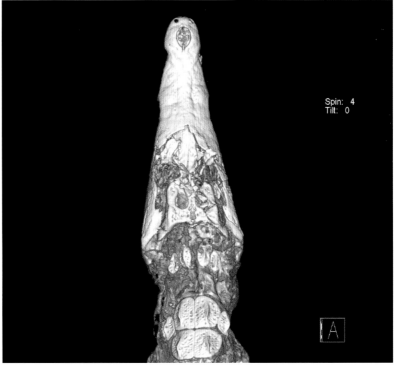

Fig. 68: Volume render of crocodile mummy (Acc. No. 1772, Manchester Museum) showing blunt force trauma to the skull vault. Render: Charlotte Brassey. Reproduced by permission of the Ancient Egyptian Animal Bio Bank, The University of Manchester.

cannot reliably suggest farming (Atherton-Woolham and McKnight 2014; Duckler and Valkenburgh 2010). Contemporary knowledge of animal husbandry shows that some animals are easier to rear and care for than others. For example, birds of prey are, to this day, notoriously difficult to rear in captivity. Based on this, it is likely that the ancient Egyptians had alternative ways and means of obtaining certain species in the numbers concerned, likely taking fledglings from the nest or capturing juveniles on their first migration (Atherton 2012).

It seems probable that the ancient Egyptians were using a combination of farmed and wild animals; both intentionally slaughtered and naturally deceased, in order to produce the volume of animal mummies witnessed in the archaeological record. It is difficult to reconcile a civilisation so observant of their environment and in whose religious beliefs animals played such a pivotal role, with the intentional demise of so many.

Treatment of animal remains during mummification

Animal remains, those intentionally killed and others who died naturally within sacred landscapes, were collected for mummification, likely by both temple staff and ordinary Egyptians (Ray 2011). There would have been great variety in the level of preservation of these remains, which in turn affected the shape of the mummy bundle.

Complete individuals mummified soon after death were generally manipulated into certain

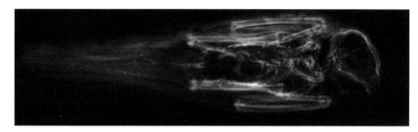
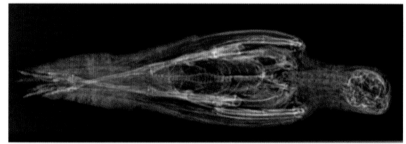
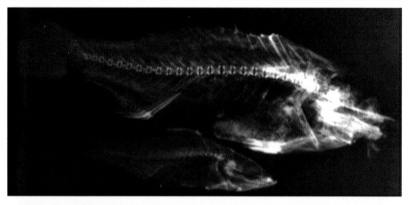
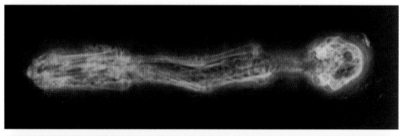
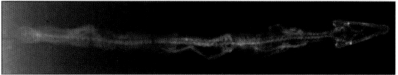

Fig. 69: Radiographs of mummies showing skeletal positions. (Acc. Nos. [top to bottom] E5408 [Garstang Museum of Archaeology], 137/1993/2 [Royal Albert Memorial Museum], E5704a [Garstang Museum of Archaeology], Ha6357 [Bristol City Museum and Art Gallery], EA19/2 [Manchester Museum]). Reproduced by permission of the Ancient Egyptian Animal Bio Bank, The University of Manchester.

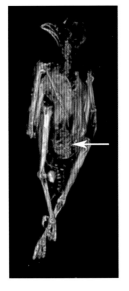
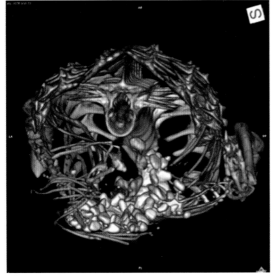

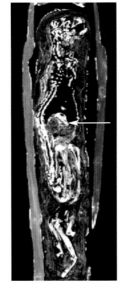
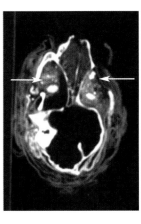

Fig. 71: Reformat of the Chester Cat (Grosvenor Museum) (left) showing a package within the abdominal cavity and transverse axial image (Acc. No. DBYMU1929-189/1, Derby Museum) (right) showing packing in the orbits. Reformats: Lidija McKnight Reproduced by permission of the Ancient Egyptian Animal Bio Bank, The University of Manchester.

Fig. 70: Reformat (Acc. No. 11295) (left) and volume render (Acc. No. 1772) (right) both from Manchester Museum showing the presence of contents within the abdominal cavities indicating that evisceration was not performed. Reformat: Lidija McKnight. Render: Charlotte Brassey. Reproduced by permission of the Ancient Egyptian Animal Bio Bank, The University of Manchester.

anatomical positions, which allowed the creation of standardised bundle forms (Fig. 69). The majority of mammals (cats and dogs) have the rear limbs flexed up, the forelimbs down and the tail curled up between the hind limbs to produce a 'skittle'-shaped bundle (Zivie and Lichtenberg 2005, 116). However, some have been found with the limbs outstretched and, in some cases, individually wrapped (Zivie and Lichtenberg 2005, 116–7). Ibises were positioned as though seated with the head either tucked under a wing, folded down as though sleeping so that the cervical vertebrae formed an 'S' shape, or twisted with the beak placed along the spine. Other bird species, particularly birds of prey, tend to have the wings folded in close to the chest with the legs bent at the femoral-tibiotarsal joint, or tucked underneath the torso. The head faces in a variety of directions: forward, left and right, as well

as forced down upon the furcula (wishbone). Crocodiles and fish were commonly presented in a natural anatomical position within longitudinal bundles; and rodents and snakes were often curled to form amorphous bundles.

Evisceration, the removal of the internal organs, and excerebration, the removal of the brain, are commonly expected features of ancient Egyptian mummification (Aufderheide 2003; Cockburn et al. 1998; David 2000, 372–89; Ikram and Dodson 1998, 103–36). Radiography of human mummies allows the route through which the brain was removed (usually by breaking through the ethmoid bone, the base of the skull or the orbit) to be visualised; with the internal organs often removed through an incision in the left flank (Ikram and Dodson 1998, 103–36; Loynes 2015, 227–8). Radiography of animal mummies, however, demonstrates that

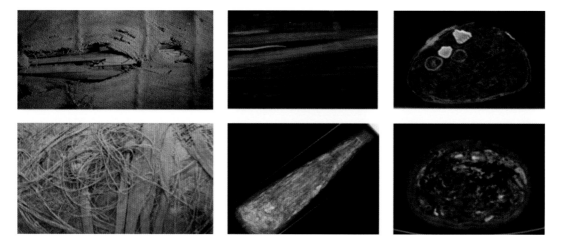

Fig. 72: Photograph, radiograph and transverse axial image (Acc. No. 15895, Kirklees Museums and Galleries) (top) showing reeds as irregular triangular structures and (Acc. No. J31.5.78.18, Museums Sheffield) (bottom) showing feathers as round, air-filled structures.

such intervention was not routine. Many animal mummies show retained cerebral matter in the cranium and the presence of desiccated viscera in the thoracic and abdominal cavities (Fig. 70). An isolated example of abdominal packing indicative of a post-mortem incision to the body was recorded on a large cat (Chester Mummy) (McKnight 2010; McKnight *et al.* in press a). This case is unusual as the complex mummification process seems to contradict the extensive post-mortem dismemberment, which allowed the bundle to fit neatly within the anthropoid wooden coffin in which it was placed (Fig. 71).

Intentionally manipulated animal remains, or those collected post-mortem for mummification, represented a considerable challenge for the embalmers. Incomplete skeletal material within mummy bundles is relatively common. It is often thought to represent 'rough-handling' during retrieval and mummification, or the result of taphonomic processes, such as disruption by predators or scavengers. Incomplete or damaged remains required a framework, or core, around which the bundle could be constructed. Evidence obtained radiographically suggests that mud, sand, plant material or linen, all of which were readily available to the embalmers, were used to fashion realistic bundle forms.

Many votive mummies contain supplementary material, intentionally or accidentally incorporated within bundles during mummification. Common materials include reed, sticks and feather, all visible radiographically as linear structures (Fig. 72). The morphology of reed and feather is easily distinguishable on transverse axial CT images, which enable visualisation of their cross-sectional form – reed is a solid, triangular structure; whereas feather demonstrates a circular, tubular appearance. The inclusions provided longitudinal form to

bundles, or acted as binding materials during the wrapping process. Isolated anomalies of unknown origin and construction are often noted. Granular inclusions are attributed to sand, stone and other inorganic debris; thought to be accidental inclusions from the embalmer's workspace.

Imaging highlights substances applied directly to the animal body and at stages throughout wrapping, visible as radiodense areas. Chemical analysis of a small number of mummy bundles demonstrated that these substances were emulsions of plant resins and beeswax in varying proportions (Buckley *et al.* 2004). It is likely that the use of such substances had both symbolic and practical motivations; as cleansing, antibacterial libations and as an adhesive to fix the linen wrappings (see Brettell 4.9 and McKnight 4.10).

Wrapping styles and decorative techniques

Animal mummies range from plainly wrapped to elaborately decorated bundles (Fig. 73). Linen fabric in a variety of weaves, colours and qualities was used, applied as shrouds or in decorative patterns, such as square and diamond lozenge, herringbone and stripes; covering the entire bundle, or forming decorative panels. A thread-like material applied either haphazardly or in an attempted pattern is noted, either as the outermost decorative layer or beneath a shroud. Often the outermost layer uses finer quality linen than the internal layers; a practice synonymous with human mummies (Riggs 2014, 113).

Decorative accoutrements, appliquéd motifs depicting divine images, are seen on conical bundles, often atop a herringbone pattern or plain shroud. Painted facial features are common in mammalian and bird mummies,

Fig. 73: Animal mummies from Manchester Museum showing the wealth of decorative techniques applied. Photo: Alan Seabright. Reproduced by permission of Manchester Museum, The University of Manchester.

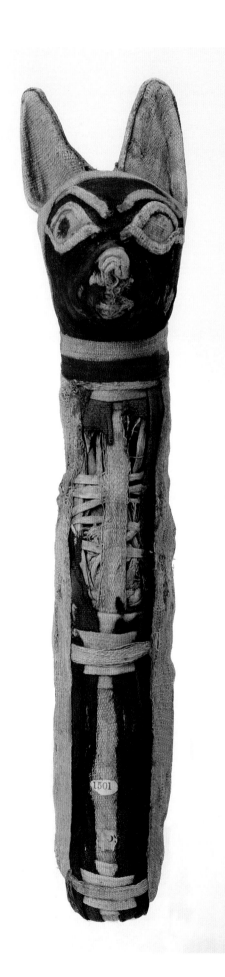

depicted in black and red paint, with linen padding creating the nose/beak, muzzle, cheeks and false ears (Fig. 74). These decorative features enable a visual association between the animal and the deity to which they were offered, and demonstrate a considerable investment of time and effort.

Imaging, aside from determining the contents of wrapped bundles, is particularly useful in demonstrating construction techniques. False heads and feet are observed, particularly in bird and mammalian mummies, to exaggerate the bundle contents with the intention of creating an elongated, anthropomorphic appearance (Fig. 75). The Osirian appearance of these bundles reinforced their purpose as an 'eternal image' of the deceased animal (Reymond 1972, 132–40).

The cross-sectional nature of CT enables linen layers to be visualised, applied at varying compressions. This suggests that wrapping took place in defined stages; perhaps even by different embalmers as part of a 'production line' with simultaneous ritual acts (Fig. 76). The technique highlights the use of linen rolls to support fragile areas of the skeleton or to create the form of pseudo-mummies and those lacking the structural integrity of a complete, articulated cadaver.

Radiography has become the 'go-to' technique for mummy studies, as an initial triage method to establish the content of wrapped bundles and to determine the mummification and wrapping techniques employed. The application of dual imaging modalities, X-ray and CT scanning, enables a comprehensive investigation at a single location, which minimises disruption to the mummies.

Fig. 74: Jackal mummy
(Acc. No. EG726, Oriental
Museum, Durham)
with false ears and
modelled facial features.
Reproduced by permission
of Durham University
Museums.

Fig. 75: Hawk mummy
(Acc. No. 1971.21,
Manchester Museum)
with false head and feet.
Photo: Alan Seabright.
Reproduced by permission
of Manchester Museum,
The University of
Manchester.

Fig. 76: Crocodile mummy
(Acc. No. 12008, Manchester
Museum) showing how
imaging can be used to
visualise unusual contents.
In total, CT highlighted four
crocodile maxilla arranged in
a line, supported by a wooden
stick, reeds and flanked by four
hatchling crocodiles. Photo:
Alan Seabright. Reformats:
Lidija McKnight and Suzie
Crimmins. Reproduced by
permission of Manchester
Museum and the Ancient
Egyptian Animal Bio Bank, The
University of Manchester.

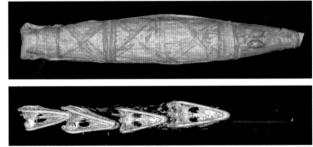

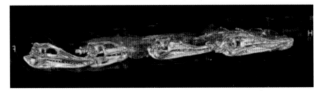

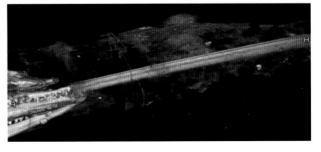

In the Industrial Setting

4.6 Industrial imaging

Lidija McKnight and Richard Bibb

Clinical radiography can pose problems when imaging archaeological specimens, mainly because the equipment is designed for use on living patients and can react unfavourably when expected to deliver high radiation doses. Industrial techniques, such as micro-CT which has the capacity for higher radiation doses, can offer increased clarity. Producing digital images with pixel size in the micrometre range (Saab *et al.* 2008, 29), this technique enables small artefacts, the content of which is often unidentifiable using clinical imaging, to be visualised in greater detail. Micro-CT is only suitable for small artefacts, up to around the length of a human femur in one scan, making the technique inappropriate for complete human mummies, but useful in the study of mummified animals, which generally fall within this size range. Size limitation is due to micro-CT scanners being sealed units with a defined field of view. Larger artefacts can be imaged using a custom bay facility, which can physically accept such specimens; however, the field of view remains unchanged so the artefact must be scanned in segments. These can be reassembled, but data alignment and the huge file sizes generated, make the process challenging.

In September 2014, five mummy bundles from Manchester Museum were selected for study using micro-CT at the Manchester X-Ray Imaging Facility, The University of Manchester. Previous clinical DR and CT imaging of two of the bundles highlighted the presence of tiny, unidentifiable bone fragments. Micro-CT demonstrated that they did in fact contain complete skeletons: one of an immature bird (Fig.77) and another of a hatchling crocodile.

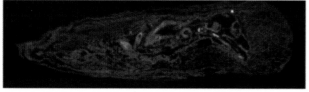

Fig. 77: 'Canine' mummy (Acc. No. 6034, Manchester Museum) believed to contain unidentifiable bones when radiographed; however, micro-CT study revealed the presence of a complete, small bird. Photo: Alan Seabright. Render: Thomas O'Mahoney. Arrangement: Lidija McKnight. Reproduced by permission of Manchester Museum and the Ancient Egyptian Animal Bio Bank, The University of Manchester.

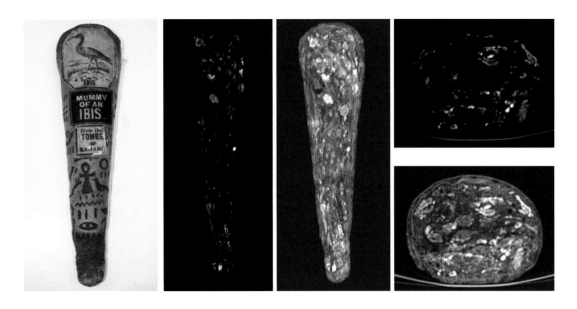

Fig. 78: 'Ibis' mummy (AEABB517, Perth and Kinross Council) showing the increased clarity offered by thresholding (from left, second and fourth image, bone window, third and fifth image, lung window). Photo and reformats: Lidija McKnight Reproduced by permission of the Ancient Egyptian Animal Bio Bank, The University of Manchester.

Image manipulation (clinical and industrial CT)

X-rays are two-dimensional images, which require little in the way of manipulation to visualise content. In contrast, CT, both clinical and industrial, produces an enormous amount of data in the form of Digital Imaging and Communications in Medicine (DICOM) files, or as a TIFF file stack. These files require sufficient computer capacity and appropriate software to visualise and manipulate the data into a useable format. Post-processing is time consuming and requires an experienced eye. Manipulation allows structures within small wrapped bundles to be viewed with ease, which is particularly valuable when aiming to identify anomalies and improve visualisation of the mummification methods employed.

Volume rendering, used frequently in clinical radiography, records the attenuation value of a selected tissue type above and below the linear attenuation co-efficient measurement of distilled water (at a standard temperature and pressure). This is defined as zero Hounsfield Units (HU) and air is defined as -1000HU (Feeman 2010). Desiccated mummified tissues, such as soft tissue, muscle and layers of treated linen, demonstrate an appearance similar to that of bone, making separation and visualisation of structures difficult. Research at Manchester has shown that bone and lung rendering thresholds, available as preset protocols on clinical scanners, are most successful on animal mummies (Fig. 78) (McKnight et al. in press b). Image data can be manually edited to delete unwanted structures and obtain 'clean' objects (Bibb et al. 2015, 450–57); however, this is extremely time consuming and requires good anatomical knowledge.

3D printing

3D printing, previously known as Rapid Prototyping, and sometimes referred to as Additive Manufacturing, is the collective name given to a variety of automated manufacturing processes that produce physical models from three-dimensional computer models, in a layer-by-layer manner. The various processes differ in the material deposited (plastics or metals) and the method of deposition.

In the late 1990s, software developments enabled the translation of 3D CT images into three-dimensional computer models that could then be transferred to 3D printing processes. This became known as medical modelling and has since become widely used in a variety of medical applications, such as the planning of complex surgeries, and the design and manufacture of custom-fitting prostheses (Bibb et al. 2015, 99–465). The same process has more recently been applied to archaeological material.

Modelling (Fig. 79) (Bibb et al. 2015, 35–64; Gibson 2002) begins with segmentation of the scan data acquired through either clinical CT or micro-CT. Segmentation involves isolating individual anatomical structures according to the greyscale (HU) value of the CT data. In CT images, higher densities appear whiter and lower densities darker; for example, bones and teeth appear white, whilst air is black and soft tissues are varying shades of grey. By assigning upper and lower thresholds, structures with specific densities can be isolated. After thresholds have been applied, individual structures can be isolated using a process called region growing. This involves selecting one pixel from within a target structure; the software then

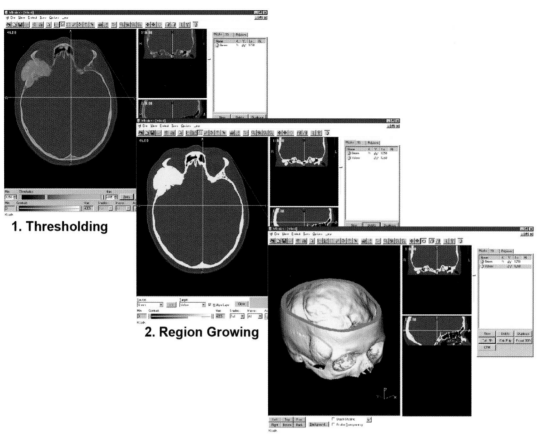

1. Thresholding

2. Region Growing

3. 3D Reconstruction

Fig. 79: Medical Modelling data segmentation steps. Reproduced by permission of Richard Bibb.

selects only those directly connected to the originally selected pixel.

Once the desired structure has been isolated, the data can then be translated into a three-dimensional computer model (Bibb *et al.* 2015, 35–64; Gibson 2002). This involves creating smooth contours for each data slice by interpolating the boundaries of the selected pixels. 3D printing processes vary in how they deposit their layers. Some use precision controlled extrusion, some use lasers to cure resins and some use ink jet style printing heads. Typically the resolution of the machines is higher than the pixel resolution of CT images, so the software interpolates smooth contours for each CT image based on the tissue density selected. In addition, 3D printing processes manufacture models in layers much thinner than the intervals between the original CT images (ranging from 0.2 to 0.016 mm); therefore the software interpolates intermediate layers to produce smooth models. When creating models of anatomy the interpolation, which follows a cubic curve, is generally highly accurate. However, errors can occur where structures are smaller than the distance between adjacent CT scan images. The 3D model can then be exported in

a format suitable for 3D printing (commonly as STL files).

Software developments and techniques have subsequently been applied to CT data acquired from ancient Egyptian mummies, enabling the manufacture of accurate physical replicas of objects found within mummy wrappings. When compared to medical modelling for clinical applications, working with CT data from mummified remains poses some distinct challenges. The main issues are caused by the desiccation of soft tissues, which results in much higher densities than found in living tissues. In many cases, the densities of desiccated soft tissue remains can approach those of the adjacent bones. This makes the automated process of region growing inaccurate. The effect of using typical region growing functions on ancient Egyptian remains can be clearly seen in Figure 80, which shows data from the mummy Tayesmutengebtiu ('Tamut', Acc. No. EA 22939) produced in collaboration with John Taylor at The British Museum. However, careful manual editing of the data combined with a sound anatomical knowledge enables the data for a given anatomical structure to be achieved.

Other concerns involve the placement of

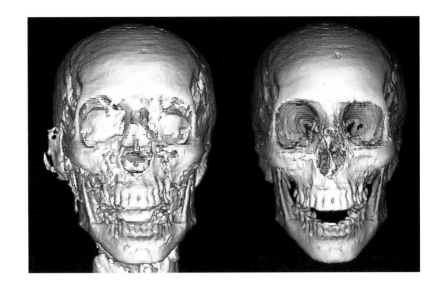

Fig. 80: The effect of region growing (left) and manually edited data (right). Reproduced by permission of Richard Bibb and the Trustees of the British Museum.

Fig. 81: Artefacts in a CT image caused by gold crowns. Reproduced by permission of Richard Bibb.

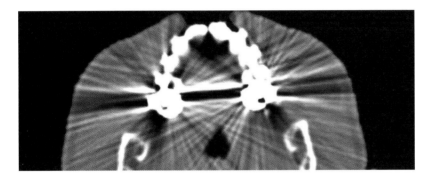

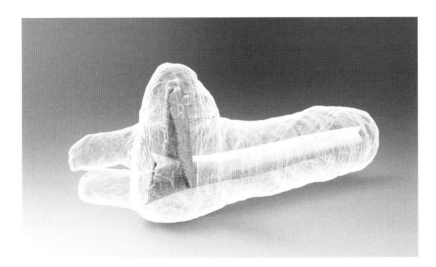

Fig. 82: Computer rendering showing the bones in relation to the wrappings. 'Jackal' mummy (Acc. No. TWCMS:2001.406, Sunderland Museum). Reproduced by permission of Richard Bibb.

objects in and around the body that may affect the quality of the scan data. Very dense objects, especially those with sharp corners, can scatter the X-rays used in CT scanning leading to false data, usually referred to as artefacts. These appear as bright streaks in the data making accurate segmentation in that area impossible (Fig. 81). Manual editing can be used to clean up the data; however, this is based on the estimation of the operator. The other potential issue involves the physical size of the remains. Scanning an entire human body plus a cartonnage container approaches the physical limits of the CT scanner. The X-rays need to penetrate not only the entire width of the body but also the additional wrappings, plus any cartonnage or coffin present. This leads to 'noise' in the data, which has a less well-defined appearance making edges and density thresholds more difficult to identify (Bibb *et al.* 2015, 450–57).

Mummified animal remains represent ideal candidates upon which to experiment with 3D printing technology due to their small size. In addition, the difficulties in identifying certain species and anomalies may be overcome using 3D printing as opposed to clinical radiography (McKnight *et al.* 2015) (Fig. 82).

For archaeology, high quality, industrial standard Additive Manufacturing machines enable precise, and academically useful, exhibition standard reproductions of objects and remains; as in, for example, the recent recreation of the remains of King Richard III by Loughborough University (Appleby *et al.* 2014). Suitably robust models make excellent teaching, handling and display aids for use in education or museum exhibits.

In the Laboratory

4.7 Sample acquisition: why, when and how is it conducted?

Lidija McKnight and Stephanie Atherton-Woolham

The acquisition of samples as part of the Ancient Egyptian Animal Bio Bank project aims to investigate the materials used in animal mummification; a somewhat neglected field with the exception of a few topical studies (Buckley 2004) (see Brettell 4.9). This procedure can be conducted at the museum for mummies unable to travel for radiographic imaging; or at Manchester after radiographic study. The ability to acquire samples is by no means a 'given' due to the excellent level of preservation of many mummy bundles (Fig. 83). However, loose associated debris, 'mummy dust' and mummy bundles in a poor or damaged state, allow removal of material with no detrimental effect (Fig. 84).

Samples are removed using tweezers, cleaned using liquid alcohol (e.g. ethanol or isopropyl), and are placed in glass jars with Teflon™-coated lids or baked aluminium foil packets to reduce plasticisation of the sample (Fig. 85). Lab coats and nitrile gloves are worn at all times, with gloves changed between mummy bundles. Safety glasses and disposable masks are worn to avoid particle inhalation in the case of bundles with high levels of 'mummy dust'.

Fig. 83: Beautifully decorated cat mummy with square lozenge linen design and modelled facial features (Acc. No. 6293, Manchester Museum). Photo: Alan Seabright. Reproduced by permission of Manchester Museum, The University of Manchester.

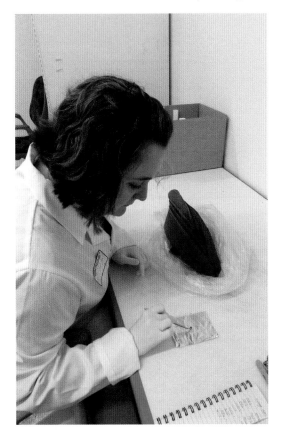

Fig. 84: Extensively damaged bird mummy showing the type of bundle from which samples can be removed (Acc. No. 2003-269, Kirklees Museums and Galleries). Photo: Lidija McKnight.

Fig. 85: Removing samples from an ibis mummy. Photo: Lidija McKnight.

Samples are visually identified, to the best of our ability, during this procedure; essentially this is an educated estimate based on their appearance and location within the mummy bundle. Sample types include linen, feather, fur, bone, skin and other soft tissues, alongside 'resinous' substances (in isolation or attached to other sample types), insect remains and the ubiquitous 'mummy dust'. Many samples however, are referred to as 'unknown'. The mummification procedure employed many different materials of animal, mineral and vegetable origin, which became compressed and have, over time, combined into a single mass, indeterminable to the naked eye.

Samples are stored in the Tissue Bank, an environmentally-monitored room designated for the storage of mummified remains. Jars are labelled and organised in order based upon their Bio Bank number within museum-grade cabinets.

4.8 What *is* that sample? Light microscopy as a screening method

Stephanie Atherton-Woolham

Before a sample can be used to answer a particular scientific question, it is vital that it is screened using non-destructive techniques to glean as much information as possible without causing unnecessary damage. Animal mummies (and the samples acquired from them) are a finite resource and require a process to be followed whereby simple questions, such as *what is this sample? what is the level of preservation?* and *is it treated with an embalming substance?* are answered first. This approach allows a good level of understanding regarding the nature of the sample and its suitability for further, destructive investigation (see Brettell 4.9). Light microscopy is able to offer this in a time- and cost-effective manner.

Several samples, identified as 'feather', were selected for screening using light microscopy. Their appearance and placement within the mummy bundle indicated that they were most likely to be feather, but the dark colouration and presence of several other materials including linen, 'resinous' and unidentifiable substances, did not allow a positive macroscopic identification. The light microscope uses light from the electromagnetic spectrum to magnify images of a sample placed in the focal plane, therefore enabling a more accurate identification. This technique is frequently used in ornithology, particularly for species identification where zooarchaeological inquiry is inconclusive (Dove 1997; Dove and Peurach 2002; Dove *et al.* 2005). Its application to ancient Egyptian votive bird feather, however, is not well known. Preliminary research at The University of Manchester has shown that it is an effective and non-destructive screening technique for investigations of embalming substances used in animal mummification (Atherton 2012).

Ideally, samples should be mounted on a glass slide, fixed using a mounting medium and covered with a transparent slip to minimise refraction. As mummified samples often merit repeat analysis, a temporary mounting method is desirable over this permanent preparation. Simply placing the sample directly on a glass slide proved adequate.

Several illumination techniques are available and it is advisable to begin with bright field. This technique transmits visible light through the sample (i.e. illuminated from below and observed from above) and is useful for highlighting untreated samples, noticeable by their transparency (Fig. 86). This technique is also able to visualise lighter coloured substances applied to the sample, in particular amber coloured coatings thought to be 'resinous' in origin (Fig. 87). However, the use of bright field on some coated samples resulted in an opaque image from which no further information could be obtained (Fig. 88, left). In these instances, reflected light, which reflects an image off the sample surface, is the next logical technique. This highlighted a viscous, often black, coating (Fig. 88, right) thought to represent a 'bituminous' substance.

Further information about the coatings on the feather samples included adhesive properties in their liquid form, which enabled attachment to the feather during mummification. In addition, the substances only coated one side of most samples, meaning that they were highly viscous when liquid, which paralleled the embalming substance created during experimental mummification (see McKnight 4.10). Over time, these properties resulted in the coating becoming brittle and breaking away from the feather, as the mummy bundle

Fig. 86: Identified as feather, this sample was untreated, noted by its transparency. Kestrel mummy (Acc. No. A957, Manchester Museum) (bright field x 20). Reproduced by permission of Stephanie Atherton-Woolham.

Fig. 87: This amber coloured coating was thought to be 'resinous' and was relatively light in its application, hence why bright field was effective. Small hawk species (Acc. No. 6095, Museum of Fine Arts, Boston) (bright field x 10). Reproduced by permission of Stephanie Atherton-Woolham.

was transported, unwrapped or moved in any way (Fig. 89).

Light microscopy helps to match the appropriate research question with the best samples to answer it, and should therefore be the first method used on this material. The use of untreated samples in a study of mummification substances, for example, would be futile. Thus, the technique acts as a proxy between sample preservation and destructive analyses.

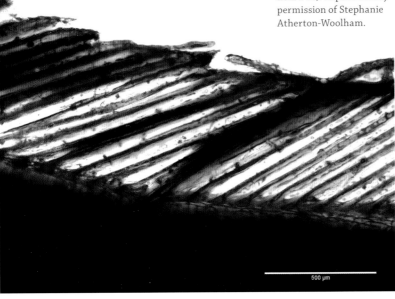

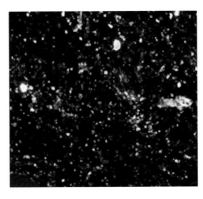

Fig. 88: Bright field proved ineffective with some coated samples and resulted in an opaque image (left). Reflected light however, demonstrated that such coatings were thick and black in colouration, thought to be bituminous (right). Bird of prey (Acc. No. 2003-269, Kirklees Museums and Galleries) (left: bright field x10; right: epipolarised light x5). Reproduced by permission of Stephanie Atherton-Woolham.

Fig. 89: Many substances were adhesive in nature at the time of application enabling them to stick to the feather (or other material). Over time however, these coatings became quite brittle, resulting in fracture and separation from the feather. Small hawk species (Acc. No. 6095, Museum of Fine Arts, Boston) (bright field x 10). Reproduced by permission of Stephanie Atherton-Woolham.

4.9 Molecular characterisation of natural products

Rhea Brettell

The natural products employed in mummification were key to its success in both physical and ritual terms (Bauman 1960; El Mahdy 1989, 11–13). Ancient texts, however, provide little information about the organic substances selected and this is particularly true in relation to animal mummies (Dunand and Lichtenberg 2006, 108–11). Likewise, chemical analysis of organic residues associated with votive mummy bundles has rarely been undertaken despite the 'unparalleled opportunities' offered by the vast numbers extant (Aufderheide 2003, 404). This is, in part, due to the considerable analytical challenge presented by the array of substances available to Egyptian embalmers (Lucas and Harris 1962, 303–37). Limitations of sample size, the potential for contamination, and the impact of both anthropogenic and environmental degradation, must also be considered. Thus, to date, the only detailed publication is that of Buckley *et al.* (2004). Their analysis of four votive mummies showed that a blend of fats/oils, beeswax and plant exudates had been applied to a cat bundle, but that bird species had received less elaborate treatments.

New research programmes, such as those conducted by the Brooklyn Museum (Bruno 2013), and the current collaborative project between the Universities of Manchester and Bradford, are now seeking to address these issues (Brettell *et al.* in review). Our approach has grown out of previous work using non-invasive techniques for the analysis of votive mummies (McKnight 2010; McKnight and Atherton 2014; McKnight *et al.* in press b) and the recovery of lipid biomarkers from comminuted grave deposits (Brettell *et al.* 2015). These studies have shown that, due to the march of time and handling of mummy bundles, small portions frequently become detached (Fig. 90). In the past, such scraps were often discarded as they could not be reattached in any meaningful manner, although it is now common practice to preserve these as part of a museum collection. The molecular characterisation of these resin fragments, balm-impregnated textiles and residue-coated feathers and other materials has, however, enormous potential for unravelling the complexities of embalming.

This has been demonstrated through the analysis of 27 samples from 18 votive mummy bundles (Fig. 91). These were initially screened using attenuated total reflectance Fourier transform infrared spectroscopy (ATR-FT-IR) to determine the class of any organic matter present. Those of consequence were then solvent extracted and derivatised (trimethylsilylated) for analysis by gas chromatography-mass spectrometry (GC-MS). Samples of varying mass and type were investigated in order to establish a sampling protocol. This was a key objective as the materials available often comprised of residual traces adhering to substrates of varying density. Recommendations regarding dimensions (i.e. 1 cm^2 of impregnated textiles) as well as mass have, therefore, been made. An assessment of the impact of solvent extraction upon these substrates was also undertaken and showed that intricate structures, such as textiles and feathers, remained intact for restoration to the contributing museums (Fig. 92).

The main aim was to determine the level of information that could be obtained from these 'mummy dust' samples, in order to formulate new research questions. The nature, range and relative abundance of the compounds identified revealed the presence of animal fats (probably intrinsic in origin), vegetable oils, plant waxes, beeswax, bitumen and plant exudates. The latter comprised of conifer – Pinaceae and perhaps Cupressaceae – products, highly degraded

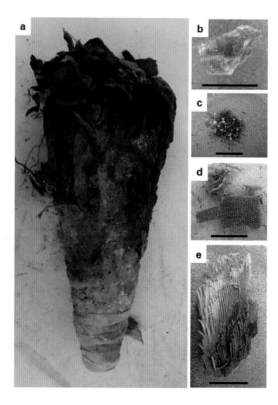

Fig. 90: Representative samples selected for analysis from votive mummies: a. damaged area of 'bird' mummy (Acc. No. 6113, Museum of Fine Arts, Boston); b. resin fragment (Acc. No. EG727, Oriental Museum, Durham); c. 'mummy dust' (Acc. No. 1910.4, Elgin Museum); d. residue-impregnated textile (Acc. No. 2003-269, Kirklees Museums and Galleries); e. residue-coated feather (Acc. No. 6095, Museum of Fine Arts, Boston) detached from mummy bundles. Scale bar = 1 cm. Reproduced by permission of Rhea Brettell.

Species / Period	AEABB number	Sample description and context	Institution details
Dog/Jackal *?Ptolemaic*	001	Linen & debris - loose in tissue paper	Grantham Museum, Grantham, UK
Cat	144	Debris - loose in box	Nottingham Castle Museum, Nottingham, UK
Cat	150	Translucent fragments + linen removed from bag of debris	Derby Museum & Art Gallery, Derby, UK
Cat	191	Linen & debris from head - sweepings	Bristol Museum & Art Gallery, Bristol, UK
Cat	595	Debris from neck region - loose in tissue paper	Old Speech Room Gallery, Harrow School, Harrow, UK
Bird of prey	004	Dark-stained linen - loose in bag and on bundle	Kirklees Museum Batley, UK
Falco **sp.**	027	Dark-stained linen - debris within tissue paper	Garstang Museum, University of Liverpool, Liverpool, UK
Hawk	146	?Black substance from rear aspect - area of damage	Nottingham Castle Museum, Nottingham, UK
Bird of prey *Late period*	153	Stained tail feathers - exposed distal end	Royal Albert Memorial Museum, Exeter, UK
Accipter **sp.**	384	Feathers with coating - left shoulder + wing	Museum of Fine Arts, Boston, USA
Bird of prey	475	Stained tail feathers - exposed inner and outer layers	New Walk Museum, Leicester, UK
Ibis *Roman*	162	Resin fragments + ?charred matter - loose from foot area	Oriental Museum, Durham University, Durham, UK
Ibis *Ptolemaic*	165	Debris – removed from packaging	Oriental Museum, Durham University, Durham, UK
Ibis *Ptolemaic/Roman*	464	Debris from head end - loose in wrappings	Buckinghamshire Museum, Aylesbury, UK
Ibis *Ptolemaic/Roman*	465	Linen & debris - loose under abdomen	Buckinghamshire Museum, Aylesbury, UK
Ibis	494	Debris - loose in tissue paper	Plymouth City Museum, Plymouth, UK
?Ibis	471	Debris from base - loose after photography	Elgin Museum, Elgin, Scotland, UK
?Bird *Ptolemaic/Roman*	401	Dark material with feather and textile impressions	Museum of Fine Arts, Boston, USA

Fig. 91: Table providing details of the votive mummy bundles sampled. Reproduced by permission of Rhea Brettell.

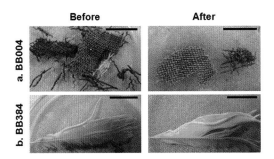

Fig. 92: Votive mummy bundle substrates before and after solvent extraction showing maintenance of their integrity: a. textile fragments (Acc. No. 2003-269/BB004, Kirklees Museum); b. feather (Acc. No. 6095/BB384, Museum of Fine Arts, Boston). Scale bar = 1 cm. Reproduced by permission of Rhea Brettell.

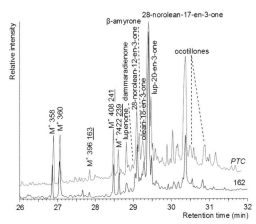

TIC (26-32 min): triterpenic compounds indicative of *Pistacia* spp. resin

Fig. 93: Biomarkers indicative of the use of a *Pistacia spp.* resin in the treatment of a votive ibis (EG727, Oriental Museum, Durham). Total ion current chromatograms (TIC), trimethylsilylated solvent extract of: a. dark amorphous mass from the foot area of the ibis; b. naturally aged modern *Pistacia terebinthus* resin from Cyprus. Reproduced by permission of Rhea Brettell.

Pistacia spp. resins (Fig. 93) and possible traces of a gum/gum-resin. These findings closely reflect the variety of natural substances previously observed in the treatment of human mummies (e.g. Buckley and Evershed 2001; Colombini *et al.* 2000; Jones *et al.* 2014), other votive animals (Buckley *et al.* 2004; Bruno 2013) and even victual offerings (Clark *et al.* 2013). In this instance, however, the most complex mixtures appear to have been used in the preparation of bird, rather than cat, mummy bundles.

Thus, molecular characterisation of this neglected resource can provide valuable insights into the treatment of votives without causing additional damage to the bundles. This paves the way for a systematic investigation of votive bundles with the potential to illuminate aspects of both life and death in ancient Egypt. These considerations range from an appreciation of the technological ingenuity and knowledge of material properties demonstrated by the Egyptians, to information relating to trade routes and tribute relations. Once an extensive database has been compiled, questions regarding the differential treatment of species and areas of the bundle, together with variations in the recipes used by different temple-based embalming workshops, can be addressed. As a result, symbolic associations between attributes such as texture, colour and scent, and the diachronic and synchronic patterning of ritual action, could be evaluated. Ultimately, research of this nature should serve to elucidate the intriguing relationship between the Egyptians, their animals and their gods.

4.10 Making mummies: experimental mummification

Lidija McKnight

Previous experiments used animal cadavers as substitutes to investigate human mummification (Garner 1979, 19–24; Lucas 1962, 289–94), rather than focusing on how animals themselves were preserved by the ancient Egyptians. More recent experiments selected animal species that were readily available (rabbits, ducks and fish) testing a wide range of materials and methods known from various animal mummy types (Clifford and Wetherbee 2004, 64-7; Ikram 2005, 16-43). These experiments, although valuable, are not entirely accurate models for votive animal mummification as they used species, techniques and ingredients inconsistent with the mummy record. Such assumptions often include evisceration, and the application of natron, a naturally occurring sodium compound, as a desiccant.

Imaging carried out at Manchester on votive animal mummies suggests that these techniques were not routinely conducted. Rather it frequently highlighted the *presence* of organs and their contents in the thoracic and abdominal cavities; direct proof that evisceration was not always practised. The ancient Egyptians would have witnessed that the bodies, many of them small, seemed to preserve perfectly well without this labour-intensive treatment, therefore enabling a more efficient production process. Research, to date, further supports the lack of a direct application of natron to the animal body, and that the majority of animal cadavers were likely to have desiccated naturally as the result of environmental conditions.

Using this evidence, experiential mummification, experiments that attempted to replicate the ancient method, were conducted. Cadavers of two small birds of prey, a Sparrowhawk (Atherton and McKnight 2014) and a Kestrel, were obtained from the Natural History Museum Bird Group in Tring. Both were dry frozen on receipt and were donated to the project for experimental purposes. Importantly these bird species have been identified in the mummy record.

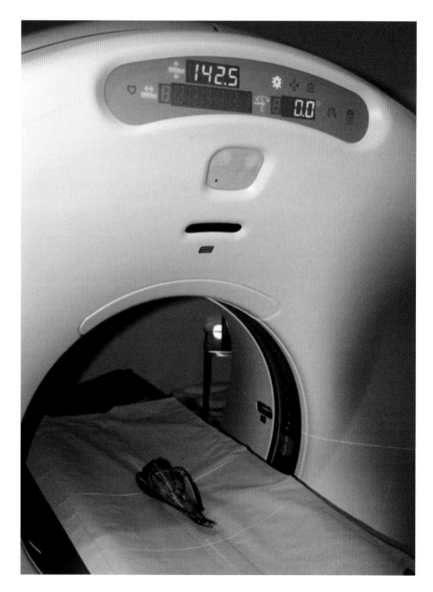

Fig. 94: Kestrel on the CT scanner gantry. Photo: Lidija McKnight.

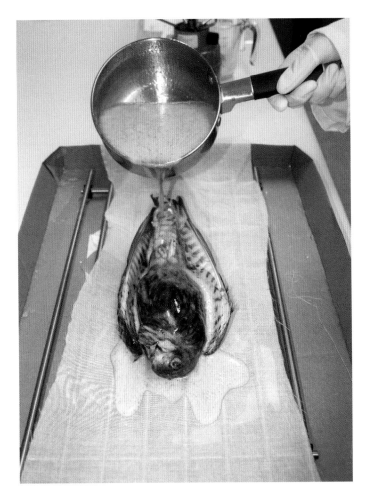

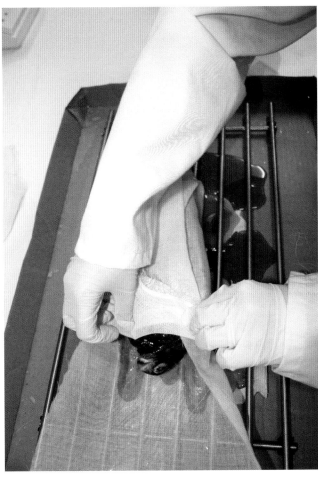

Fig. 95: Pouring the resin:beeswax emulsion over the breast of the Kestrel. Photo: Lidija McKnight.

Fig. 96: Wrapping the anointed Kestrel in linen. Photo: Lidija McKnight.

Clinical imaging, carried out at the Central Manchester University Hospital NHS Foundation Trust, was employed prior to and after mummification as an assessment tool (Fig. 94). This enabled the differentiation between ante- and peri-mortem markers, such as cause of death or pathology; and post mummification, in particular fractures caused through handling the cadaver. In addition, it highlighted variation in mummification practice such as the presence of abdominal contents.

The experiments used a very basic mummification 'recipe'. First, the cadavers were thawed and placed in an incubator in an attempt to mimic the environmental conditions of the Egyptian desert. Their weight was recorded during every stage of the process, as was the humidity and temperature in the fume cupboard where the mummies were housed. Evisceration was not practised and no desiccant was applied. Instead, an 80:20 emulsion of pine resin:beeswax, previously identified through the analysis of linen samples from a bird mummy provenanced to Tarkhan (Buckley *et al.* 2004), was manufactured. The emulsion was poured, with particular attention to the breast

region, where it pooled in the area enclosed by the wings in their resting, anatomical position (Fig. 95); this phenomenon has been observed as a radio-opacity in ancient mummies. Pre-cut linen strips were used to wrap the coated cadavers (Fig. 96).

A number of observations were made during the process. Firstly, the application of the molten emulsion was rather unpleasant, not only due to the difficulty of manipulating a hot, sticky cadaver, but also because it exacerbated the malodour. Manoeuvring the cadaver during wrapping also proved awkward. As layers of linen were applied to cover the treated cadaver, it became increasingly easy to apply further strips of linen and affix the loose edges with dabs of the resin:beeswax substance; much in the same manner as the ancient embalmers.

Once mummification was complete, repeat imaging was performed which confirmed that, in both cases, mummification did not cause any fractures. Wrapping caused the skulls to lie in unusual positions, which has been recorded in many ancient mummies where it appears to lie at an uncomfortable angle in relation to the body, or has been forced downwards,

93

shortening the cervical spine and causing the head to rest directly on top of the furcula (wishbone). Furthermore, the wrapping of the modern cadavers was noticeably less compressed than the ancient examples. During the CT scanning of ancient mummies clearly defined stages of linen application were visible, usually two or three, at different compressions within the bundle.

Imaging, over a period of two years, showed that the muscle mass of the cadavers decreased steadily and that abdominal contents, visible as opacities on pre-mummification images, began to desiccate and recede from the cavity walls (Fig. 97). These observations, along with the encouraging overall weight loss of the bundle, suggest that the experiments continue to be effective.

Zooarchaeologists rely on the direct comparison of physical skeletal remains in order to aid identification. This is complicated when bones are not directly visible because they are wrapped within mummy bundles. To explore this problem, eight cadavers (road and pet kill) were experimentally mummified using the same technique with the aim of improving our knowledge of the identification of animals using imaging alone (Fig. 98). This is a notoriously difficult task, particularly in the case of birds where morphological differences are slight. Once desiccated, the experimental mummy bundles will be dissected. This will allow comparison between the imaging results and the use of zooarchaeological methods, thereby determining how accurately we can identify animal remains in ancient mummy bundles.

When experiments began, it was unknown as to whether a preserved animal mummy could be made in a cold, humid Manchester laboratory. Over three years have passed and the mummies remain stable, suggesting that the arid Egyptian climate was not imperative for bodily preservation. Future experiments on bird cadavers will assess the maximum body mass before which evisceration becomes necessary to achieve preservation. Analysis of mummification materials removed from the bodies (rather than the wrappings) of ancient votive mummies (see Brettell 4.9) will be used to further evaluate votive animal mummy recipes, which will allow further experimental recreation.

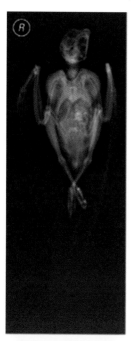
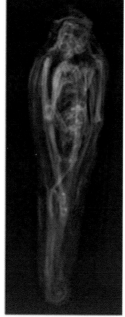
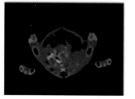

Fig. 97: Left to right – AP radiographs and transverse axial CT slices taken prior to mummification (left) and six months post mummification (right). These images chart the change from the plump cadaver pre-mummification to the desiccation of the soft-tissue on the limb bones and the shrinkage of the visceral contents from the abdominal walls. Arrangement: Lidija McKnight.

Fig. 98: The Manchester experimental mummies. Photo: Lidija McKnight.

Back at the Museum
4.11 Museum-researcher relationships
Lidija McKnight

When animal mummy research began at Manchester, it quickly became clear that many museums were unaware of the potential value of their mummified material. The reasons behind this are complex: either that mummified material was outside the scope of their display and was relegated to the stores; that the economic climate had caused staff shortages and made research on the collections untenable; or simply that the current staff members were unaware of such material in the collection at all. Mummies have come to light in the most surprising places around Britain and the mere fact that an external researcher enquired into the possibility of a collection containing such material, was often enough to prompt staff to go in search of mummies in the dark depths of the stores. This is by no means a criticism of museums or their staff; it is simply a reflection of the climate faced by museums today.

A vital element of the Bio Bank project is to encourage people to see the potential value of mummified animal remains, both in terms of what they can tell us about the ancient civilisation that created them, but also what they can teach us about the history of science and our own attitudes to cultural heritage. Visitors to museums will always be interested in mummies, but our challenge is to promote understanding and offer new evidence capable of challenging existing preconceptions.

A large-scale research project such as the Bio Bank encourages small regional museums to participate in collaborative research. In exchange for support and access, museums are able to learn about their collections and draw comparisons with other institutions. Access to resources, which would normally fall outside of their scope, often encourages participation and it is important the results of any analysis conducted is communicated quickly and efficiently. This information is used to update records, inform learning programmes, supplement displays and determine conservation. The Bio Bank project believes that it has fashioned a legacy, both in the creation of an atmosphere of shared knowledge between museums and researchers, and between museums and their visitors. Perhaps the most important legacy is the protection of the material and our ability to help museums to ensure the survival of the resource for the benefit of future generations.

4.12 Conservation and care of animal mummies

Sam Sportun

The conservation department at Manchester Museum is responsible for the care of a wide variety of artefacts, amongst which mummified remains constitute some of the most fragile. At first glance the animal mummies on display appear to be in remarkably good condition, considering their age and the inevitable ordeals of their journey from Egypt to Manchester. Once leaving their deposition site, their journey would have involved an animal drawn cart, a sea voyage to Britain and then, most likely, a train or canal barge to Manchester. This is in marked contrast to our meticulous packing and careful transportation of collections today, to avoid even the smallest vibration that may put the object at risk of damage.

Animal mummies come in a wide range of configurations and consist mainly of organic material. This includes textiles (commonly linen made from flax fibres), skeletal remains and preserved soft tissues, anomalous material, and mummification substances (Buckley and Evershed 2001) (see Brettell 4.9). Pseudo animal mummies are formed from a variety of non-skeletal materials including reeds, wooden sticks, feathers, eggshell, sand and mud within textile wrappings. This variety means there are several factors we must consider when caring for animal mummies. Maintaining a pest free, stable environment (constant temperature and humidity at 40–55%) is vital to ensure that the

mummies are not affected by damp, which in turn can cause fungal and bacterial growth, and lead to deterioration and staining.

Textiles are vulnerable to light damage; however, when animal mummies were first displayed for public viewing at Manchester they were placed in cases with exposure to daylight (Fig. 99). Redevelopment of the gallery in the 1980s rectified this and natural light was eliminated. Daylight is the most common source of ultraviolet light, a wavelength particularly damaging to organic material, so care should be taken to avoid any exposure to direct and indirect sunlight, when possible. Exposure to ultraviolet light weakens the structure of linen/flax fibres, causing them to break and lose structural integrity.

Individual assessment of each artefact determines the level of physical support required, either for display purposes or when in storage. All mummies are susceptible to damage during movement or from inappropriate pressure to the surface of the artefact. Wrappings are often fragile and brittle, especially where fragments have become loose and exposed, which can lead to the unravelling of bindings and exposure of the bundle contents, in turn affecting their cohesion.

A number of animal mummies in the collection have lost their wrappings at some time and the animal remains have become exposed.

Fig. 99: The Manchester Museum galleries in 1928. Reproduced by permission of Manchester Museum, The University of Manchester.

Fig. 100: Decorative detail on an ibis mummy (Acc. No. 11501, Manchester Museum) picked out on accent on applique with dark coloured textile. Reproduced by permission of Manchester Museum, The University of Manchester.

Fig. 101: Crocodile mummy showing the deterioration of the dark linen wrappings (Acc. No. 12008, Manchester Museum). Photo: Sam Sportun.

Scientific analysis of small samples removed from mummies has identified numerous resins and waxes used during the mummification process, including pine and conifer resins, beeswax, gum resin and bitumen (Buckley and Evershed 2001) (see Brettell 4.9). Exposure of bundle contents can reveal these coatings, such as on the large Manchester crocodile (Acc. No. 1772) where the liberal application of resin has stiffened and offers protection and rigidity to the mummy's form. In some areas the brittle coating has loosened the skin, putting it at risk of becoming detached (see Atherton-Woolham 4.8). Ensuring adequate support along the length of the bundle, rather than simply laying them in a drawer or box, can prevent this damage, especially in the case of lengthier bundles where their size increases the risk of bending.

The majority of the mummies are wrapped in un-dyed linen, ranging in both colour and friability. Some mummies have decorative features accentuated with darker, dyed linen. Ascertaining the original colour can be difficult due to discoloration and deterioration of the fibres. Dark textiles are used to depict details such as eyes on the pseudo hawk (Acc. No. 11293), appliqué design on the ibis (Fig. 100) (Acc. No. 11501), or as part of an intricate woven design on the bird mummy (Acc. No. 11296). Dark linen is noticeably more friable than the surrounding linen, which can become weakened as a result of its proximity to the dark linen. Iron compounds in textile dyes are known to negatively affect the cellulose fibres in the long term, causing them to break down (Bruno 2013, 113–14). The crocodile mummy (Acc. No. 12008) clearly demonstrates this phenomenon (Fig. 101).

Conservation involves the cleaning and stabilisation of weakened material elements which may be at risk of further deterioration. If necessary, the surface is cleaned with a low-suction vacuum and a soft-bristled brush. Fragile linen wrappings on animal mummies can be stabilised to prevent further loss. Textile creases are eased by the controlled introduction of moisture, taking particular care taken not to let humidity affect any surrounding areas. The loose wrappings can then be returned to their correct alignment. Encasing the affected area with fine colour-matched nylon gauze gently and securely holds bindings in place and does not exert undue pressure on extraneous, frayed or brittle linen strands. Stitching the nylon gauze to itself rather than to the ancient textile is the accepted method to avoid undue damage. Wrappings can be secured by attaching them to

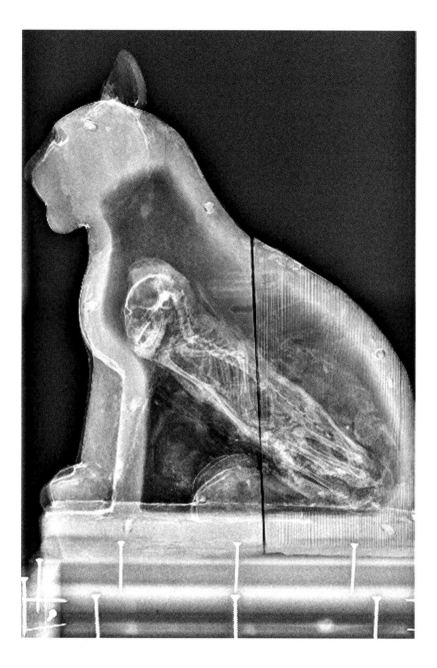

Fig. 102: Radiograph of a mummified cat in a wooden coffin (Acc. no. 9303a-b, Manchester Museum) showing the relationship between the different elements (skeleton, wrappings and wooden outer coffin). Reproduced by permission of the Ancient Egyptian Animal Bio Bank, The University of Manchester.

colour-matched strips of soft Japanese paper using a weak reversible adhesive that provides physical support for fraying fibres.

Understanding the structural integrity of each animal mummy is vital to ensuring their long-term care, display and storage. Radiographic imaging allows assessment of the content of wrapped bundles and determines their susceptibility to movement, deterioration and pressure; especially important if the object is to be loaned outside of the institution. The relationship between a mummy bundle and its surroundings can be further complicated by the addition of a container such as in the case of Manchester's cat in a wooden coffin. (Acc. No. 9303a-b) (Fig. 102). Anomalous inorganic material, such as stone and metal amulets,

would pose a further conservation concern; however, none of the animal mummies within the Manchester collection show evidence of such inclusions. Information gathered through radiographic investigation has enabled individual conservation plans to be developed, based not only upon the visual appearance of mummies, but on their contents. Display and storage concerns have been tailored to suit specific mummies based upon the results of scientific investigation.

There is still much to learn from these enigmatic artefacts and advances in non-invasive analytical techniques continue to expand our understanding of their manufacture and use, and allow us, as custodians, to care for them in the most appropriate fashion.

Epilogue

Researching animal mummification is, undeniably, an exciting job. Using non-invasive imaging techniques to see inside mummy bundles for the first time since they were wrapped over 2000 years ago, is an incredible privilege. Perhaps the most satisfying is being involved in such a truly inter-disciplinary field with the opportunity to work closely with specialists and museum professionals. For museums trusted with safeguarding heritage, this has been an obvious and mutually beneficial relationship – without access to collections there is no research project, yet without research helping to better inform collections management, there is no longevity for the collection itself.

The incorporation of new disciplines, many of which have benefited from their involvement in the study of animal mummies, often starts out as mere curiosity for how applicable a particular technique is to material of this kind. Working with specialists experienced in their chosen field provides a very different, but often highly informative, dimension to research, and as a result, the Bio Bank protocol is constantly evolving. More recently, samples from the Bio Bank have been used in ancient DNA and proteomic analysis. However, a fail-safe method for their application is yet to be determined, primarily due to the great variation in preservation witnessed in mummified samples.

There can be little doubt that mummies – human and animal – have much to thank modern science for; however, in return, science owes a debt of gratitude to mummies. They represent a medium upon which to test and develop new technologies, and broaden our comprehension of the capabilities of modern methods to enhance our understanding of the past.

Ancient Egypt and mummies in particular, have, and will always be, a crowd-pleaser, but the ability to better understand collections through new and exciting scientific research, brings these ancient artefacts into the twenty-first century. The use of non- or minimally-invasive techniques must remain our primary objective. Museums are custodians of material heritage, yet historians and scientists also play an important role in the search for knowledge and the ongoing preservation of the material.

We hope that this book, and the exhibition that shares its name, are able to make a positive contribution to mummy research and inspire the general public, the academic community and future generations of researchers, keen to unravel the mysteries of animal mummies.

We are conscious that our work at Manchester is a drop in the ocean and that there is much still to be discovered, yet we hope that what we have achieved is to make a valuable contribution to this area of study. It seems fitting to conclude with the words of Amelia Edwards, a pioneering woman in the field of Egyptology, both in Egypt and at home in Britain. Her words ring true over a century later when we find ourselves faced with a subject which has lost none of its appeal, yet which promises everything to those willing to search, and question, the material remains of this fascinating culture.

> *Thus the work of discovery goes on apace. Old truths receive unexpected corroboration; old histories are judged by the light of new readings; fresh wonders are disclosed wherever the spade of the digger strikes new ground. The interest never flags – the subject never palls upon us – the mine is never exhausted.*

(Edwards 1891, 4)

*Lidija McKnight and
Stephanie Atherton-Woolham*

Bibliography

Abdallah, A. O. A. 1992. *Graeco-Roman Funerary Stelae from Upper Egypt*. Liverpool: Liverpool University Press.

Adams, B. 1987. *The Fort Cemetery at Hierakonpolis*. London: Kegan Paul International.

Adams, B. 1995. *Ancient Nekhen: Garstang in the City of Hierakonpolis*. New Malden, Surrey: SIA.

Adams, A. L. 1864. 'Notes on the Mummied Bodies of the Ibis and Other Birds found in Egypt', *Edinburgh New Philosophical Journal*, 19, 173–83.

Adams, J. E. and Alsop, C. W. 2008. 'Imaging in Egyptian Mummies', in. A. R. David (ed.), *Egyptian Mummies and Modern Science*. Cambridge: Cambridge University Press.

Alberti, S. 2009. *Nature and Culture: Objects, Disciplines and the Manchester Museum*. Manchester: Manchester University Press.

Aldred, C. and Sandison, T. 1961. 'The Tomb of Akhenaten at Thebes [and appendix]', *Journal of Egyptian Archaeology*, 47, 41–65.

Allan, D. 1941. 'The Destruction of the Liverpool City Museums: A Review of Events', *Museums Journal*, 41, 105–7.

Appleby, J., Mitchel, P. D., Robinson, C., Brough, A., Rutty, G., Harris, R. A., Thompson, D. and Morgan, B. 2014, 'The scoliosis of Richard III, last Plantagenet King of England: diagnosis and clinical significance', *The Lancet*, 383 (9932), 1944.

Anderson, J. 1898. *Zoology of Egypt*. London: Bernard Quaritch.

Anon. 1821. 'Egyptian Antiquities', *Kaleidoscope*, 8 May, 342.

Armitage, P. L. and Clutton-Brock, J. 1981. 'A radiological and historical investigation into the mummification of cats from ancient Egypt', *Journal of Archaeological Science*, 8 (2), 185–96.

Assmann, J. 2001. *The Search for God in Ancient Egypt*. Ithaca: Cornell University Press.

Atherton, S. D. 2012. *An investigation of the post-mortem status and mummification practices of avian votive mummies in ancient Egypt*. Unpublished Ph.D. Thesis, University of Manchester.

Atherton, S. D., Brothwell, D. B., David, R. A. and McKnight, L. M. 2012. 'A healed femoral fracture of *Threskiornis aethiopicus* (Sacred Ibis) from the Animal Cemetery at Abydos, Egypt', *International Journal of Paleopathology*, 2, 45–7.

Atherton, S. D. and McKnight, L. M. 2014. 'The mummification of votive birds: past and present', *EXARC Journal*, 2014/1. Available at: http://journal.exarc.net/issue-2014-1/ea/mummification-votive-birds-past-and-present.

Aufderheide, A. C. 2003. *The Scientific Study of Mummies*. Cambridge: Cambridge University Press.

Bacon, E. 1967a. 'The quest for Imhotep', *The Illustrated London News*, 25 March 1967, 30.

Bacon, E. 1967b. 'Saqqara: the clues mount up in the quest for Imhotep', *The Illustrated London News*, 29 July 1967, 23–5.

Bacon, E. 1967 *c*. 'Saqqara: the evidence of the treasure of Imhotep', *The Illustrated London News*, 5 August 1967, 25–7.

Baha el-Din, S. 2012. 'The Avifauna of the Egyptian Nile Valley: Changing Times', in R. Bailleul-LeSuer (ed.), *Between Heaven and Earth: Birds in Ancient Egypt*. Chicago: The University of Chicago.

Baines, J. 2000. 'Egyptian Deities in Context: Multiplicity, Unity and the Problem of Change', in B. N. Porter (ed.), *One God or Many? Concepts of Divinity in the Ancient World*. Casco Bay Assyriological Institute, 9–78.

Baumann, B. B. 1960. 'The Botanical Aspects of Ancient Egyptian Embalming and Burial', *Economic Botany*, 14 (1), 84–104.

Belzoni, G. 1820. *Plates illustrative of the researches and operations of G. Belzoni in Egypt and Nubia*. London: John Murray.

Berger, J. 1980. *Why look at animals?* Pantheon: New York.

Bibb, R., Eggbear, D. and Paterson, A. 2015. Medical Modelling: the application of advanced design and development techniques in medicine. 2nd edition. Cambridge: Elsevier (Woodhead).

Bleiberg, E. 2013. 'Animal Mummies: The Souls of the Gods', in E. Bleiberg, Y. Barbash and L. Bruno (eds), *Soulful creatures: Animal mummies in ancient Egypt*. Brooklyn, NY: Brooklyn Museum and Giles Ltd, 63–105.

Bleiberg, E., Barbash, Y., and Bruno, L. (eds), 2013. *Soulful creatures: Animal mummies in ancient Egypt*. Brooklyn, NY: Brooklyn Museum and Giles Ltd.

Boni, T., Rühli, F. J., and Chlem, R. K. 2004. 'History of paleopathology: early published literature, 1896–1921', Journal of the Canadian Association of Radiology, 55 (4), 211–17.

Bresciani, E. 2005. 'Sobek, Lord of the land and the lake', in S. Ikram (ed.), *Divine Creatures: Animal mummies in ancient Egypt*. Cairo: The American University in Cairo Press.

Brettell, R. C, Schotsmans, E. M. J., Walton Rogers, P., Reifarth, N., Redfern, R. C., Stern, B. and Heron, C. P. 2015. '*Choicest Unguents*: Molecular Evidence for the Use of Resinous Plant Exudates in Late Roman Mortuary Rites in Britain', *Journal of Archaeological Science*, 53 (January), 639–48.

Brettell, R. C., Atherton-Woolham, S. D., Martin, W. H. C., Stern, B. and McKnight, L. M. in review. 'Unparalleled opportunities: organic residue analysis of Egyptian votive mummies and their research potential', submitted to Studies in Conservation.

Brewer, D. J. and Friedman, R. F. 1989. *Fish and Fishing in Ancient Egypt*. Warminster: Aris and Phillips.

Brocklehurst, M. 2004. *Miss Brocklehurst on the Nile: Diary of a Victorian Traveller in Egypt*. Stockport: Millrace.

Bruno, L. 2013. 'The Scientific Examination of Animal Mummies', in E. Bleiberg, Y. Barbash and L. Bruno (eds), *Soulful Creatures: Animal Mummies in Ancient Egypt*. Brooklyn, NY: Brooklyn Museum and Giles Ltd, 108–37.

Buckley, S. A. and Evershed, R. P. 2001. 'Organic Chemistry of Embalming Agents in Pharaonic and Graeco-Roman Mummies', *Nature*, 413 (6858), 837–41.

Buckley, S. A., Clark, K. A. and Evershed, R. P. 2004. 'Complex organic chemical balms of Pharaonic animal mummies', *Nature*, 431 (7006), 294–9.

Butzer, K. 1976. *Early hydraulic civilisation in Egypt: A study in cultural ecology*. Chicago: University of Chicago Press.

Campbell, C. 1914. *Guide to the Egyptian Antiquities in Kelvingrove Art Gallery and Museum, Glasgow*.

Glasgow: Robert Anderson.

Clark, K. A., Ikram, S. and Evershed, R. P. 2013. 'Organic Chemistry of Balms used in the Preparation of Pharaonic Meat Mummies', *PNAS*, 110 (51), 20392–5.

Clifford, W. and Wetherbee, M. 2004. 'Making a Duck Mummy and Discovering a Secret of the Ancient Technology', *KMT: a modern journal of ancient Egypt*, 15 (2), 64–7.

Cockburn, A., Cockburn, E. and Reyman, T. A. 1998. *Mummies, Disease and Ancient Cultures*. Cambridge: Cambridge University Press.

Colombini, M. P., Modugno, F., Silvano, F. and Onor, M. 2000. 'Charaterisation of the Balm of an Egyptian Mummy from the Seventh Century B.C.', *Studies in Conservation*, 45, 19–29.

Contis, G. and David, A. R. 1996. 'The Epidemiology of Bilharzia in Ancient Egypt: 5000 Years of Schistosomiasis', *Parasitology Today* 12 (7), 253–5.

Cornelius, I., Swanepoel, L. C., du Plessis, A. and Slabbert, R. 2012. 'Looking inside votive creatures: computed tomography (CT) scanning of ancient Egyptian mummified animals in Iziko Museums of South Africa: a preliminary report', *Akroterion*, 57, 129–48.

David, A. R. (ed.), 1979. *The Manchester Museum Mummy Project. Multidisciplinary Research on Ancient Egyptian Mummified Remains*. Manchester: Manchester University Press.

David, A. R. 1986. *The Pyramid Builders of Ancient Egypt*. London and New York: Routledge.

David, A. R. and Tapp, E. (eds), 1992. *The Mummy's Tale*. London: Michael O'Mara Books Limited.

David, A. R. 2000. 'Mummification', in P. T. Nicholson and I. Shaw (eds), *Ancient Egyptian Materials and Technology*. Cambridge: Cambridge University Press, 372–89.

David, R. (ed.) 2008. *Egyptian Mummies and Modern Science*. Cambridge: Cambridge University Press.

Davies, S. and Smith, H. S. 2005. *The Sacred Animal Necropolis at North Saqqara: The Falcon Complex and Catacomb: The Archaeological Report*. London: Egypt Exploration Society.

Davies, S. 2006. *The Sacred Animal Necropolis at North Saqqara: The Mother of Apis and Baboon Catacombs: The Archaeological Report*. London: Egypt Exploration Society.

Davies, S. 2007. 'Bronzes from the Sacred Animal Necropolis at North Saqqara' in M. Hill (ed.), *Gifts for the Gods. Images from Egyptian Temples*. New York: Metropolitan Museum of Art, 174–87.

Dawson, W. R. and Gray, P. H. K. 1968. *Catalogue of Egyptian Antiquities in the British Museum, volume 1. Mummies and human remains*. London: The Trustees of the British Museum.

Dawson W. and E. Uphill. 1972. *Who Was Who in Egyptology*. 2nd Edition. London: Egypt Exploration Society.

Dawson, W. R. and E. P. Uphill. 1995. *Who was who in Egyptology*. 3rd Edition. London: Egypt Exploration Society.

De Meulenaere, H. 1990. 'Bronzes égyptiens de donation', *Bulletin des Musées Royaux d'Art et d'Histoire*, 61, 63–81.

De Meulenaere, H. 1992. *Ancient Egypt in Nineteenth Century Painting*. Berko.

De Meulenaere, H. 1993. 'Les antiquités Égyptiennes de la collection Charles Bogaert', *Bulletin de la Société Française d'Égyptologie*, 127, 6–19.

De Morgan, J. 1897. *Carte de la Nécropole de la Memphite: Dahchour, Sakkarah, Abou-Sir*. Cairo: Institut Français de l'Archéologie Orientale.

Description de l'Egypte. 1809. Paris: Pancoucke.

Dodson, A. 2005. 'Bull cults', in S. Ikram (ed.), *Divine Creatures: Animal Mummies in Ancient Egypt*. Cairo: American University in Cairo Press, 72–105.

Dove, C. J. 1997. 'Quantification of microscopic feather characters used in the identification of North American plovers', *The Condor*, 99 (1), 47–57.

Dove, C. J. and Peurach, S. C. 2002. 'Microscopic analysis of feather and hair fragments associated with human mummified remains from Kagamil Island, Alaska', in W. S. Laughlin, B. Fröhlich, A. B. Harper and R. Gilbert (eds), *To the Aleutians and Beyond – The Anthropology of William S. Laughlin*. National Museum of Denmark, 51–62.

Dove, C. J. Hare, P. G. and Heacker, M. 2005. 'Identification of ancient feather fragments found in melting alpine ice patches in Southern Yukon', *Arctic*, 58 (1), 38–43.

Downes, D. 1974. *The Excavations at Esna 1905–6*. Warminster: Aris & Phillips Ltd.

Drew-Bear, M. 1979. *Le Nome Hermopolite: Toponymes et sites*. Missoula, Montana: Scholars Press.

Ducker, L. and Valkenburgh, B. V. 2010. 'Exploring the health of late Pleistocene mammal: the use of Harris lines', *Journal of Vertebrate Paleontology*, 18 (1), 180–8.

Dunand, F. and Lichtenberg, R. 2006. *Mummies and Death in Egypt*, trans. D. Lorton. Ithaca & London: Cornell University Press.

Eaton-Krauss, M. 2008. 'Embalming Caches', *Journal of Egyptian Archaeology*, 94, 288–93.

Edwards, A. B. 1877. *A Thousand Miles Up The Nile*. London: Routledge and Sons.

Edwards, A. B. 1888. 'The provincial and private collections of Egyptian antiquities in Great Britain', *Recueil de Travaux*, 10, 121–33.

Edwards, A. B. 1891. *Pharaohs, Fellahs and Explorers*. New York: Harper and Brothers.

El Mahdy, C. 1989. *Mummies, Myth and Magic in Ancient Egypt*. London: Thames and Hudson.

Emery, W. B. 1965a. Preliminary report on the excavations at North Saqqâra 1964–5. *Journal of Egyptian Archaeology*, 51, 3–8.

Emery, W. B. 1965b. 'The search for Imhotep in Sakkara', *The Illustrated London News*, 6 March 1965, 20–3.

Emery, W. B. 1967. 'Preliminary report on the excavations at North Saqqâra 1966–7', *Journal of Egyptian Archaeology*, 53, 141–5.

Emery, W. B. 1969. 'Preliminary report on the excavations at North Saqqâra 1968', *Journal of Egyptian Archaeology*, 55, 31–5.

Emery, W. B. 1970. 'Preliminary report on the excavations at North Saqqâra 1968–9', *Journal of Egyptian Archaeology*, 56, 5–10.

Emery, W. B. 1971. 'Preliminary report on the excavations at North Saqqâra 1969–70', *Journal of Egyptian Archaeology*, 57, 3–13.

Eyre, C. 2013. 'Women and Prayer in Pharaonic Egypt', in E. Frood and A. McDonald (eds), *Decorum and Experience. Essays in Ancient Culture for John Baines*. Oxford: Griffith Institute, 109–16.

Fagan, B. *The Rape of the Nile. Tomb Robbers, Tourists and Archaeologists in Egypt*. New York: Scribner.

Feeman, T. G. 2010. *The Mathematics of Medical Imaging: A Beginner's Guide*. Berlin, Heidelberg: Springer-Verlag.

Forbes, H. 1907. *Fifty-Fourth Annual Report of the Committee of the Free Public Museums of the City of Liverpool for the year ending 31st December, 1906*. Liverpool: C. Tinling & Co.

Friedman, R. and Buck, P. 2008. 'Tell el-Ahmar, Tell el-Baqliya, Tell el-Naqus: Supplementary information on the Tell Baqliya cluster', in *The Egypt Exploration Delta Survey: An information centre for the archaeological sites of lower Egypt*. London: Egypt Exploration Society. Online version: http://www.deltasurvey.ees.ac.uk/ds-home.html [Accessed 30 August 2008].

Garner, R. 1979. 'Experimental Mummification', in A. R. David (ed.), *The Manchester Museum Mummy Project: multidisciplinary research on ancient Egyptian mummified remains*. Manchester: Manchester University Press, 19–24.

Garnett, A. 2015. 'John Rankin and John Garstang: Funding Egyptology in a Pioneering Age', in P. Piacentini, C. Orsenigo and S. Quirke (eds), *Forming Material Egypt: Proceedings of the International Conference*, London, 20–21st May 2013, EDAL IV, 95–104.

Garnett, A., Ollett, C. and Laycock, G. 2011.

'From Egypt's Sands to Northern Hills: John Garstang's Excavations in Egypt', *Ancient Egypt Magazine*, 12 (2), 34–7.

Garstang, J. 1907a. *The Burial Customs of Ancient Egypt. As illustrated by Tombs of the Middle Kingdom, being A Report of Excavations made in the Necropolis of Beni Hassan during 1902–3–4.* London: Archibald Constable and Co. Ltd.

Garstang, J. 1907b. 'Excavations at Hierakonpolis, at Esna and in Nubia', *Annales du Service des Antiquitiés de l'Egypte*, 8, 132–48.

Gatty, C. 1879. *Catalogue of the Mayer Collection Part I. The Egyptian, Babylonian, and Assyrian Antiquities*, 2nd Edition. London: Bradbury, Agnew, & Co.

Gaunt, J., 2005. *Corpus Vasorum Antiquorum (21, Harrow School).* Oxford: Oxford University Press.

Gibson, M. and Wright, S. (eds), 1988. *Joseph Mayer of Liverpool 1803–1886.* London: Society of Antiquaries in association with the National Museums & Galleries on Merseyside.

Gibson, I. 2002. *Software Solutions for Rapid Prototyping.* Oxford: Wiley-Blackwell.

Gray, P. H. K. 1966. 'Radiological aspects of the mummies of ancient Egyptians in the Rijksmuseum van Oudheden, Leiden' Reprinted from *Oudheidkundige mededelingennuit het Rijksmuseum van Oudheden, Leiden*, 47.

Gray, P. H. K. 1973. 'The radiography of mummies of ancient Egyptians', *Journal of Human Evolution*, 2, 51–3.

Gray, P. H. K. and Slow, D. 1968. *Egyptian Mummies in the City of Liverpool Museums.* Liverpool: Liverpool Cooperation.

Grenfell, B., Hunt, A. and Smyly, J. G. 1902. *The Tebtunis papyri: Part I.* London: Egypt Exploration Fund.

Haddon, K. 1914. 'Report on a Small Collection of Mummy Dogs', in Naville (ed.), *The Cemeteries of Abydos. Part I – 1909–1910. The Mixed Cemetery and Umm el Ga'ab.* London: The Egypt Exploration Fund.

Harris, H. A. 1933. 'Rickets', in *Bone Growth in Health and Disease, Oxford Medical Publications.* London: Oxford University Press.

Hart, G. 1986. *Egyptian Gods and Goddesses.* London: Routledge and Kegan Paul.

Harwood-Nash, D. C. F. 1979. 'Computed tomography of ancient Egyptian mummies', *Journal of Computer Assisted Tomography*, 3, 768–73.

Hoath, R. 2003. *A Field Guide to the Mammals of Egypt.* Cairo. The American University in Cairo Press.

Holland, T. 1937. 'X-rays in 1896', *Journal of Liverpool Medico-Chirurgical Society,* 45, 61.

Hollings, M. A. (ed.), 1917. *The life of Sir Colin C. Scott-Moncrieff.* London: J. Murray.

Hounsfield G. N. 1973. 'Computerized transverse axial scanning (tomography). 1. Description of the system', *British Journal of Radiology*, 46 (552), 1016–22.

Ikram, S. and Dodson, A. 1998. *The Mummy in Ancient Egypt: Equipping the Dead for Eternity.* London: Thames and Hudson.

Ikram, S. 2003. 'The Animal Mummy Project at the Egyptian Museum Cairo', in Z. Hawass, (ed.), *Egyptology at the Dawn of the Twenty-first Century: Proceedings of the Eight International Congress of Egyptologists, Cairo 2000.* Cairo: American University Press in Cairo, 235–9.

Ikram, S. 2005. *Divine Creatures: Animal Mummies in Ancient Egypt.* Cairo: The American University Press in Cairo.

Ikram, S. 2007. 'Animals in the Ritual Landscape at Abydos: A Synopsis', in Z. Hawass and J. Richards (eds), *The Archaeology and Art of Ancient Egypt.* Cairo: Supreme Council of Antiquities.

Ikram, S. 2013. 'A Curious Case of Canine Burials at Abydos', in M. C. Flossmann-Schütze, M. Goecke-Bauer, F. Hoffmann, A. Hutterer, A. Schütze and M. Ullmann (eds), *Kleine Götter – Grosse Götter: Festschrift für Dieter Kessler zum 65. Geburtstag.* Munich: Verlag Patrick Brose.

Ikram, S., Nicholson, P. T., Bertini, L. and Hurley, D. 2013. 'Killing man's best friend?' *Archaeological Review from Cambridge*, 28, 2, 48–66.

Isherwood I., Jarvis H. and Fawcitt R. A. 1979. 'Radiology of the Manchester mummies', in A. R. David (ed.), *The Manchester Mummy Project: Multidisciplinary Research on Ancient Egyptian Mummified Remains.* Manchester, Manchester University Press, 25–64.

Jeffreys, D. G. and Smith, H. S. 1988. *The Anubieion at Saqqara.* London: Egypt Exploration Society.

Jones, J., Higham, T. F. G., Oldfield, R., O'Connor, T. P. and Buckley, S. A. 2014. 'Evidence for Prehistoric Origins of Egyptian Mummification in Late Neolithic Burials', *PLoS ONE,* 9 (8), e103608.

Kavanagh, G. 1994. *Museums and the First World War: A Social History.* London: A & C Black.

Kemp, B. 1982. 'Abydos', in T. G. H James (ed.), *Excavating in Egypt. The Egypt Exploration Society in Egypt 1882–1982.* Chicago and London: The University of Chicago Press.

Kessler, D. 1986. 'Tierkult', in W. Helck, E. Otto and W. Westendorf (eds), *Lexikon der Ägyptologie*, 6, 517–87. Wiesbaden: O. Harrassowitz.

Kessler, D. and Nur el-Din, A. H. 2005. 'Tuna al-Gebel: Millions of Ibises and other animals', in S. Ikram (ed.), *Divine Creatures: Animal Mummies in Ancient Egypt.* Cairo: The American University in Cairo Press, 120–63.

Koenig, W. 1896. *14 Photographien mit Rontgen-Strahlen aufgenommen im Physikalischen Verein zu Frankfurt-am-Main.* Leipzig: Johann Ambrosius Barth.

Lambert-Zazulak P., Rutherford, P., David, R. 2003. 'The International Ancient Egyptian Mummy Tissue Bank at the Manchester Museum as a resource for the palaeoepidemiological study of Schistosomiasis'. *World Archaeology,* 35 (2), 223–40.

Larson, F. 2009. *An Infinity of Things: How Sir Henry Wellcome collected the world.* Oxford: Oxford University Press.

Loat, W. L. S. 1913. 'The Ibis Cemetery', in T. E. Peet and W. L. S. Loat (eds), *The Cemeteries of Abydos. Part III – 1912–1913.* London: The Egypt Exploration Fund.

Loynes, R. 2015. 'Prepared for Eternity. A study of human embalming techniques in ancient Egypt using computerised tomography scans of mummies'. BAR Egyptology, 9. Oxford: Archaeopress.

Lucas, A. and Harris, J. 1962. *Ancient Egyptian Materials and Industries,* 4th Edition, revised. London: Edward Arnold.

Mariette, A. 1857. *Le Sérapeum de Memphis découvert et décrit par Auguste Mariette.* Paris: Gide.

Mariette, A. 1869–80. *Abydos: description des fouilles exécutées sur l'emplacement de cette ville.* Paris: Imprimerie Nationale.

Martin, G. T. 1973. 'Excavations in the Sacred Animal Necropolis at North Saqqâra, 1971–2: preliminary report', *Journal of Egyptian Archaeology,* 59, 5–15.

Martin, G. T. 1974. 'Excavations in the Sacred Animal Necropolis at North Saqqâra, 1972–3: preliminary report', *Journal of Egyptian Archaeology,* 60, 15–29.

Martin, G. T. 1981. *The Sacred Animal Necropolis at North Saqqara.* London: Egypt Exploration Society.

Mayer, J. 1852. *Catalogue of the Egyptian Museum, No. VIII, Colquitt Street, Liverpool.* Liverpool: Mawdsley and Son.

McKnight (née Owen), L. M. 2001. *A radiographic investigation of the ancient Egyptian animal mummies from the Manchester Museum.* Unpublished M.Sc. Dissertation, University of Manchester.

McKnight, L. M. 2010. *Imaging Applied to Animal Mummification in Ancient Egypt,* BAR International Series 2175. Oxford: Archaeopress.

McKnight, L. M., Atherton, S. D and David A. R. 2011. 'Introducing the Ancient Egyptian Animal Bio Bank at the KNH Centre for Biomedical Egyptology, University of Manchester', *Antiquity Project Gallery,* 85 (329). Available at: http://www.antiquity.ac.uk/ projgall/mcknight329. [Accessed 21 May 2015]

McKnight, L. M. and Atherton, S. D. 2014. 'How to "pigeonhole" your Mummy – a proposed categorization System for Ancient Egyptian Wrapped Animal Remains based on Radiographic Evaluation', *Yearbook of Mummy Studies,* 2. Munich: Dr Friedrich Pfeil, 109–16.

McKnight, L. M. 2015. 'The Art of Embalming – a macroscopic and radiographic evaluation of decorative techniques applied to mummified votive Egyptian mammalian remains' in M. Pinarello, J. Yoo, J. Lundock and C. Walsh (eds), *Current Research in Egyptology 2014: Proceedings of the Fifteenth Annual Symposium, UCL and KCL, April 9–12, 2014.* Oxford and Philadelphia: Oxbow Books, 239–52.

McKnight, L. M., Adams, J. E., Chamberlain, A., Atherton-Woolham, S. D. and Bibb, R. 2015. 'Application of clinical imaging and 3D printing to the identification of anomalies in an ancient Egyptian animal mummy'. *Journal of Archaeological Science: Reports,* 3, 328–32.

McKnight, L. M., Atherton-Woolham, S. D., Adams, J. E. and Price, C. In press a. 'Preliminary Research on the Chester Coffin – A Potential Case of Mistaken Identity and Coffin Reuse?' in *Proceedings of the First Vatican Coffin Conference.* Vatican City: Vatican Museum Press.

McKnight, L. M., Atherton-Woolham, S. D. and Adams, J. E. In press b. 'Clinical Imaging of Ancient Egyptian Animal Mummies', *RadioGraphics.*

Meeks, D. and Favard-Meeks, C. 1996. *Daily Life of the Egyptian Gods.* Ithaca, NY: Cornell University Press.

Moodie, R. L. 1931. 'Roentgenologic studies of Egyptian and Peruvian mummies', in B. Laufer (ed.), *Anthropology Memoirs of the Field Museum,* 3. Chicago: Field Museum of Natural History.

Moser, S. 2006. *Wondrous Curiosities. Ancient Egypt at the British Museum.* Chicago: University of Chicago Press.

Moshenska, G. 2014. 'Unrolling Egyptian mummies in nineteenth-century Britain', *The British Journal for the History of Science,* 47 (3), 451–77.

Murray, J. 1888. *A Handbook for Travellers In Lower and Upper Egypt.* London: John Murray.

Murray, M. A. 1910. *The Tomb of Two Brothers.* Manchester: Sherratt and Hughes.

Murray, M. 1912. 'Position of Women', in J. M. Buchanan (ed.), *Guide for Egyptian Research Students Association and a Catalogue of Loan Collection of Egyptian Antiquities Held in*

Kelvingrove Museum, Glasgow. Glasgow: John Smith & Son.

Naville, E. and T. E. Peet. 1910–11. 'Excavations at Abydos', *Archaeological Report (Egypt Exploration Fund)*, 1–5. London: Egypt Exploration Fund.

Newberry, P. E. 1893–4. *Beni Hasan Parts I and II*. London: Egypt Exploration Fund.

Nicholson, P. T. 2005. 'The Sacred Animal Necropolis at North Saqqara: The cults and their catacombs', in S. Ikram (ed.), *Divine Creatures: Animal mummies in ancient Egypt*. Cairo: The American University in Cairo Press, 44–71.

Nicholson, P. T. and Shaw, I. 2000. *Ancient Egyptian Materials and Technology*. Cambridge: Cambridge University Press.

Nicholson, P. T., Harrison, J. Ikram, S., Earl, E. and Qin, Y. 2013. 'Geoarchaeological and environmental work at the Sacred Animal Necropolis, North Saqqara, Egypt', in L. Marks (ed.), *The Memphite Necropolis (Egypt) in the Light of Geoarchaeological and Palaeoenvironmental Studies*. Warsaw: Studia Quaternaria, 30 (2), 83–9.

Nicholson, P.T., Ikram, S. and Mills, S. 2015. 'The Catacombs of Anubis at north Saqqara', *Antiquity*, 89, 345, 645–61.

O'Connor, D. 2009. *Abydos: Egypt's First Pharaohs and the Cult of Osiris*. London: Thames and Hudson Ltd.

Orel, S. E. 1997. 'John Garstang at Beni Hasan', *KMT: a modern journal of ancient Egypt*, 8 (1), 54–61.

Osborn, D. J. and Osbornova, J. 1998. *The Mammals of Ancient Egypt*. Warminster: Aris and Phillips.

Peet, T. E. 1914. *The Cemeteries of Abydos. Part II – 1911–1912*. London: The Egypt Exploration Fund.

Petrie, W. M. F. 1888. *Tanis II*. London: Egypt Exploration Fund.

Petrie, W. M. F. 1889. *Hawara, Biahmu and Arsinoe*. London: Field and Tuer.

Petrie, W. M. F. 1898. *Deshasheh*. London: Egypt Exploration Fund.

Petrie, W. M. F. 1900. *Denderah*. London: Egypt Exploration Fund.

Petrie, W. M. F. 1902. *Abydos I*. London: Egypt Exploration Fund.

Petrie, W. M. F. 1907. *Gizeh and Rifeh*. London: British School of Archaeology in Egypt.

Petrie, W. M. F. 1912. *The Religion of Ancient Egypt*. London: Archibald Constable and Co. Ltd, 20–27.

Petrie, W. M. F., Brunton, G. and Murray, M. 1923. *Lahun II*. London: British School of Archaeology in Egypt.

Pinch, G. 1993. *Votive Offerings to Hathor*. Oxford: Griffith Institute.

Pinch, G. and Waraksa, E. A. 2009. 'Votive Practices', in J. Dieleman, E. Frood and W. Wendrich (eds), UCLA Encyclopedia of Egyptology. Los Angeles. Available at: http://escholarship.org/uc/item/7kp4n7rk. Accessed 21 May 2015.

Pococke, R. 1743. *A Description of the East and Some Other Countries. Volume 1: Observations on Egypt*. London: W. Boyer.

Price, C. and M. Scott. Forthcoming. 'The Egyptian Collection of Max Robinow in the Manchester Museum', in R. Mazza (ed.), *From Egypt to Manchester: Special edition of the Bulletin of the John Rylands Library*.

Raven, M. and Taconis, W. K. E. 2005. *Egyptian Mummies: Radiological Atlas of the Collections in the National Museum of Antiquities in Leiden*. Brepols: Turnhout.

Ray, J. D. 1970. 'A note on "building 3"' in *Saqqara Animal Necropolis Excavation Notes, 69/70* (Currently held at the Egypt Exploration Society London Office, Doughty Mews).

Ray, J. D. 1976. *The Archive of Hor*. London: Egypt Exploration Society.

Ray, J. D. 1978. 'The World of North Saqqara', *World Archaeology*, 10 (2), 149–57.

Ray, J. D. 2011. *Texts from the Baboon and Falcon Galleries: Demotic, Hieroglyphic and Greek inscriptions from the Sacred Animal Necropolis, North Saqqara*. London: Egypt Exploration Society.

Reymond, E. A. E. 1972. 'The $s^{c}h$ "eternal image"', Zeitschrift für ägyptische sprache und altertunskunde 98, 132–40.

Riggs, C. 2014. *Unwrapping Ancient Egypt*. London: Bloomsbury.

Saab, G., Chhem, R. K. and Bohay, R. N. 2008. 'Paleoradiologic Techniques', in R. Chhem and D. Brothwell (eds), *Paleoradiology: Imaging Mummies and Fossils*. Berlin, Heidelberg: Springer-Verlag.

Said, R. 1981. *The Geological Evolution of the River Nile*. New York: Springer-Verlag.

Sampsell, B. M. 2003. *A Traveler's Guide to the Geology of Egypt*. Cairo: American University in Cairo Press.

Sampsell, B. M. 2014. *The Geology of Egypt*. Cairo: American University in Cairo Press.

Sams, J. 1839. *Ancient Egypt. Objects of Antiquity forming part of the extensive & rich collections from ancient Egypt, brought to England by & now in the possession of J. Sams*. London: J. Sams.

Sandison, T. 1963. 'The use of Natron in Mummification in Ancient Egypt', *Journal of Near Eastern Studies*, 22 (4), 259–67.

Schulz, R. 2004. 'Treasures of Bronze', *Bulletin of the Egyptian Museum*, 1, 61–6.

Shaw, I. 2000. *The Oxford History of Ancient Egypt*. Oxford: Oxford University Press.

Shaw, I. 2008. *Sir John Gardner Wilkinson, Pioneer Egyptologist, Handlist of the Harrow School Collection of Egyptian Antiquities*. Published by Harrow School.

Shaw, I. and Nicholson, P. 1995. *British Museum Dictionary of Ancient Egypt*. London: British Museum Press.

Silverman, D. P. 1991. 'Divinity and deities in ancient Egypt', in B. Shafer, J. Baines, L. H. Lesko and D. P. Silverman (eds), *Religion in Ancient Egypt: Gods, myths and personal practice*. London, Ithaca: Cornell University Press.

Smith, H. S. 1971. 'Walter Bryan Emery', *Journal of Egyptian Archaeology*, 57, 190–201.

Smith, H. S. 1974. *A Visit to Ancient Egypt. Life at Memphis and Saqqara, c. 500–30 BC*. Warminster: Aris and Phillips.

Smith, H. S. 1976. 'Preliminary report on excavations in the Sacred Animal Necropolis, season 1974–1975', *Journal of Egyptian Archaeology*, 62, 14–7.

Smith, H. S. and Jeffreys, D. G. 1977. 'The Sacred Animal Necropolis, North Saqqâra: 1975/6', *Journal of Egyptian Archaeology*, 63, 20–8.

Smith, H. S., Davies, S. and Frazer, K. J. 2006. *The Sacred Animal Necropolis at North Saqqara: The Main Temple Complex: The Archaeological Report*. London: Egypt Exploration Society.

Snape, S. R. 1985. *Mortuary Assemblages from Abydos*. Unpublished Ph.D. Thesis, The University of Liverpool.

Snape, S. R. 1994. 'Statues and Soldiers at Abydos in the Second Intermediate Period'. In C. J. Eyre (ed.), *The Unbroken Reed: Studies in the Culture and Heritage of Ancient Egypt*. London: Egypt Exploration Society.

Snape, S. 2011. *Ancient Egyptian Tombs: The Culture of Life and Death*. Chichester: Wiley-Blackwell.

Sotheby and Son, 1835. *Catalogue of the Highly Interesting and Magnificent Collection the Property of the Late Henry Salt, Esq., His Britannic Majesty's Late Consul General in Egypt*. London: J. Davy.

Spurr, S. 2000. *Egyptian Art at Eton College: Selections from the Myers Museum*. New Haven, Connecticut: Yale University Press.

Strouhal, E. 1997. *Life of the Ancient Egyptians*. Liverpool: Liverpool University Press.

Taylor, J. H. 2001. *Death and the Afterlife in Ancient Egypt*. London: British Museum Press.

Taylor, J. H. and Antoine, D. 2014. *Ancient Lives, New Discoveries: eight mummies, eight stories*. London: British Museum Press.

Teeter, E. 2002. 'Animals in Egyptian Religion', in B. J. Collins, (ed.), *A History of the Animal World in the ancient Near East*. Volume 64 of the Handbook of Oriental Studies. Boston, Köln: Brill.

Teeter, E. 2011. *Religion and Ritual in Ancient Egypt*. Cambridge: Cambridge University Press.

Thompson, J. 1992. *Sir Gardner Wilkinson and his Circle*. Austin, TX: University of Texas Press.

Tutton, A. E. H. 1932. 'Mr. Leonard Loat. Scientific Work in Many Lands', *The Times Newspaper*, 30 April 2014.

Von den Driesch, A., Kessler, D., Steinmann, F., Berteaux, V. and Peters, J. 2006. 'Mummified, deified and buried at Hermopolis Magna – the sacred birds from Tuna el-Gebel, Middle Egypt', in M. Bietak (ed.), *Ägypten und Levante*, XV: International journal of Egyptian Archaeology and Related Disciplines, 203–44.

Van de Walle, B. 1976. 'Le catalogue de la collection Ch. Bogaert', *Chronique d'Égypte*, 51, 47–57.

Waterfield, R. 1998. *Herodotus: the Histories*. Oxford: Oxford University Press.

West, J. B., Bowen, G. J., Cerling, T. E. and Ehleringer, J. R. 2006. 'Stable isotopes as one of nature's ecological recorders', *Trends in Ecology and Evolution,* 21 (7), 408–14.

West, J. B., Bowen, G. J., Dawson, T. E. and Tu, K. P. (eds), 2010. *Isoscapes: Understanding movement, pattern, and process on earth through isotope mapping*. Heidelberg, Germany: Springer Dordrecht.

Whittemore, T. 1914. 'The Ibis Cemetery at Abydos: 1914', *Journal of Egyptian Archaeology,* 1 (4), 248–9.

Wilde, W. R. 1840. *Narrative of a Voyage to Madeira, Tenerife, and along the Shores of the Mediterranean*. London: Longman, Orme, Brown and Co.

Wilkinson, J. G. 1994. *The Ancient Egyptians, their Life and Customs, I and II*. Senate Books.

Wilkinson, J. G. 1864–65. *Letters from Sir John Gardner Wilkinson to Montagu Butler, Head Master of Harrow School, dating from1864 and 1865* (Currently held in the Old Speech Room Gallery Harrow School Collection).

Wilkinson, R. 2003. *The Complete Gods and Goddesses of Ancient Egypt*. London: Thames and Hudson.

Wyatt, J. H. and Garner, J. Forthcoming. *Birds in Ancient Egypt: A Guide to Identification*.

Yallop, J. 2011. *Magpies, squirrels and thieves: how the Victorians collected the world*. London: Atlantic.

Zivie, A. and Lichtenberg, R. 2005. 'The Cats of the Goddess Bastet' in S. Ikram (ed.), *Divine Creatures: Animal Mummies in Ancient Egypt*. Cairo: The American University in Cairo Press, 106–19.

Contributor Biographies

Judith Adams

Professor Judith Adams qualified at University College Hospital London; after medical posts in Cambridge, she began her radiology career at the Manchester Royal Infirmary and The University of Manchester where she is a Consultant Radiologist and Professor of Radiology. She is a musculo-skeletal radiologist with special interests in the imaging of metabolic and endocrine diseases, in particular osteoporosis, and in quantitative methods of assessment of the skeleton, on which topics she has published widely. She has been involved in the imaging of mummies, of both humans and animals, for over twenty years and has supervised students undertaking research projects in this field.

Stephanie Atherton-Woolham

Dr Stephanie Atherton-Woolham has been part of the Ancient Egyptian Animal Bio Bank project since its inception in 2010, after studying Egyptology at the University of Liverpool and Biomedical Egyptology at The University of Manchester. Her research primarily focuses on bird mummification practices in ancient Egypt, in particular the use of imaging (both radiographic and microscopic) on museum collections. Furthermore, her interests lie in comparing radiographic results with the evolution of bird mummy wrapping techniques and styles in the Late-Roman Periods, and the development of a timeline for votive bird mummification in ancient Egypt. She is an Honorary Curator of Archaeozoology at Manchester Museum and Project Curator for the 'Gifts for the Gods' exhibition.

Rozenn Bailleul-LeSuer

Rozenn Bailleul-LeSuer is a Ph.D. candidate in Egyptology in the Department of Near Eastern Languages and Civilizations at the University of Chicago. She is currently finishing her dissertation entitled 'The Exploitation of Avian Resources in Ancient Egypt: A Socio-Economic Study'. In 2012–13 she curated the exhibit 'Between Heaven and Earth: Birds in Ancient Egypt' at the Oriental Institute Museum, Chicago. In addition to evaluating the importance of fowling and aviculture in Egyptian society, her research interests include the study of sacred bird cults, with a special focus on the scientific analysis of bird mummies.

Richard Bibb

Dr Richard Bibb graduated from Brunel University with a B.Sc. in Industrial Design in 1995 and moved to the National Centre for Product Design & Development Research (PDR), Cardiff to undertake Rapid Prototyping research. In 1998 he established the Medical Applications group at PDR to conduct research into the medical applications of design technologies, including Rapid Prototyping/3D printing. He moved to Loughborough University in 2008. His research has investigated design technologies in maxillofacial surgery, prosthetic rehabilitation, orthotics, dental technology and archaeology and has been presented in Europe, Japan, South Africa, Egypt, Canada and USA, which resulted in 80 peer-reviewed publications.

Rhea Brettell

Rhea Brettell is a business woman turned archaeological scientist. She has a B.Sc. in Archaeological Sciences and M.Sc. in Human Osteology and Palaeopathology from the University of Bradford and an M.A. in Local and Regional History from Goldsmith's College, London. After a brief sojourn teaching secondary science she seized the opportunity in 2011 to return to Bradford to take up an AHRC funded Ph.D., which combines her main interests: the molecular analysis of organic residues and ritual action in the mortuary sphere.

Don Brothwell

Professor Emeritus Don Brothwell conducts research in archaeological science at the University of York. He has worked on various Egyptian collections over the past fifty years. Recent research has included animal mummies, and aspects of their palaeopathology. He now believes that this material is a precious resource in urgent need of far more attention than it has previously achieved. Also, that research planning should be undertaken at an international level, and to include, when possible, molecular variation. Hand in hand with this, should be conservation studies to ensure the long-term preservation of these fragile tissues.

Ashley Cooke

Dr Ashley Cooke is Senior Curator of Antiquities at World Museum, National Museums Liverpool, and Honorary Research Fellow in the department of Archaeology, Classics and Egyptology at the University of Liverpool. In 2006 he received a Ph.D. in Egyptian Archaeology from University of Liverpool, having started excavating in Egypt in 1997 with field experience at Rifeh, Saqqara, Tell Abqa'in, the Valley of the Kings and Zawiyet Umm el-Rakham. He previously worked at the Garstang Museum of Archaeology at the University of Liverpool and Manchester Museum, The University of Manchester.

Rosalie David, OBE

Until 2012, Professor Emeritus Rosalie David was the first Director and Professor of Biomedical Egyptology at the KNH Centre for Biomedical Egyptology, The University of Manchester. As Director of the Manchester Mummy Research Project, she established a new university specialisation – biomedical research in Egyptology. Author/editor of over 30 books and many articles in peer-reviewed journals, she has lectured around the world, and acted as consultant and contributor for television documentaries. She is a Fellow of The Royal Society of Arts and The Royal Society of Medicine and was awarded an OBE for services to Egyptology in 2003.

Anna Garnett

Anna Garnett is Assistant Project Curator for the on-going British Museum fieldwork project at Amara West, Sudan, based in the Department of Ancient Egypt and Sudan at The British Museum. She is also a Ph.D. candidate at the University of Liverpool and the title of her thesis is '*Sacred Space and Religious Expression in Egypt's Eastern Desert*'. Her research interests include ceramics from New Kingdom Egyptian sites in Nubia, New Kingdom religious architecture, Egyptian royal sculpture and colossal statuary, and the collection and display history of British Egyptological collections.

Gabrielle Heffernan

Gabrielle Heffernan is a British Museum curatorial trainee, currently based at the Burrell Collection in Glasgow. She is also a Ph.D. candidate at the University of Birmingham, having previously completed a Master's degree at the same university and a Bachelor's degree at the University of Cambridge. Her current research focuses on memory and state legitimation in the Egyptian eighteenth Dynasty. Gabrielle has also excavated at the sites of South Asasif and Elephantine in southern Egypt.

Henry McGhie

Henry McGhie is Head of Collections and Curator of Zoology at Manchester Museum. His background is as an ornithologist, specialising in bird ecology and historical ecology. His current interests are in the development of ornithology in the nineteenth and early twentieth centuries, explored through the biography of Henry Dresser, and in exploring ways to connect museums with environmental sustainability. His work combines exhibitions, public engagement, collections development, university teaching and academic development, drawing on collections wherever possible.

Lidija McKnight

Dr Lidija McKnight holds a B.Sc. in Archaeology from the University of York and an M.Sc. and Ph.D. in Biomedical Egyptology from The University of Manchester. Since 1999, Lidija has conducted research into animal mummification, particularly through the application of non-invasive radiographic imaging. As founder of the Ancient Egyptian Animal Bio Bank, Lidija has studied numerous museum collections in Britain, Europe and the United States. She has presented and published widely on the subject and is passionate about engaging the public with the study of this material. Lidija holds the position of Honorary Curator of Archaeozoology at Manchester Museum and is Project Curator for the '*Gifts for the Gods*' exhibition.

Paul T. Nicholson

Professor Paul T. Nicholson has worked on excavations in Egypt since 1983 and has directed projects there since 1992, when he began work at the Sacred

Animal Necropolis at Saqqara alongside Professor H. S. Smith. His work at Saqqara resumed in 2009 with a new exploration of the Catacombs of Anubis at the site. As well as sacred animals, his research interests include aspects of early technology and he is co-editor (with Ian Shaw) of *Ancient Egyptian Materials and Technology* (2000), *Brilliant Things for Akhenaten* (2007) and *Working in Memphis* (2013). He is currently a Professor of Archaeology at Cardiff University, Wales.

Campbell Price

Dr Campbell Price completed his B.A., M.A. and Ph.D. in Egyptology at the University of Liverpool, where he is an Honorary Research Fellow. He has undertaken fieldwork at the sites of Zawiyet Umm el-Rakham and Saqqara, and worked in Liverpool's Garstang Museum of Archaeology. Since 2011, he has been the Curator of Egypt and Sudan at Manchester Museum. His research interests include elite culture and religious expression in Egypt during the First Millennium BC.

Samantha Sportun

Sam Sportun is Collection Care Manager and Senior Conservator at Manchester Museum having originally studied Conservation at Durham University. She has managed the Conservation Department at Manchester Museum for six years and previously ran the Sculpture Conservation Department at National Museums Liverpool, where she worked for 13 years. She has an interest in new 3D digital technologies and how they can be used to make collections more accessible, and has recently completed an M.A. in creative digital technologies.

Alice Stevenson

Dr Alice Stevenson is the Curator of UCL's Petrie Museum of Egyptian Archaeology. She has previously held research and teaching contracts at the University of Oxford's Pitt Rivers Museum, the Institute of Archaeology, UCL, and the Egypt Exploration Society. The primary sources for her research have always been museum collections and archives related to early fieldwork, through which she has explored a range of themes in prehistoric archaeology. These collections and archives have also formed departure points for her related interest in the history of the disciplines of archaeology, anthropology and museum studies.

Julia Walton

Having completed her degree in Comparative Literature at the University of East Anglia, Julia Walton joined Oxford University Press (International Division) as an editor, based in Ibadan, Nigeria. In 1983 she joined the staff of The British Museum, initially as an exhibition editor but progressing, via a two-year secondment as Assistant Director of the Museums and Galleries Commission, to the British Museum Directorate and subsequently to the Department of Greek and Roman Antiquities. In 2005 she was appointed Director of Quex Museum, House and Gardens, Kent, and took up her post as Curator of the Old Speech Room Gallery at Harrow School in 2011.

Brian Weightman

Brian Weightman gained a B.A. in Archaeology, from the Institute of Archaeology, UCL. His research interests lie in the study of ancient technologies and the role played by museum collections in education. He currently works as a Learning Assistant for Glasgow Museums.

John Wyatt

John Wyatt is an ornithologist by profession but read Anthropology at university in the then Salisbury, Southern Rhodesia. He specialises in African birds and animals but for the last ten years has been concentrating on ancient Egypt in preparation for two books on the birds and mammals thereof. He is a Research Volunteer for both the Egypt Exploration Society and the Griffith Institute, Oxford, and also a regular tour leader to Egypt. He has presented at study days, conferences, seminars and other meetings on the subject.

Concordance of mummies

This list provides the corresponding Bio Bank number and museum information relating to the mummies mentioned in this book. The identifications and provenance provided here are as they appear in the museum records. Subsequent analysis for this project may have led to revised descriptions, which can be found in the text.

Bio Bank Number	Museum Number	Holding Museum	Recorded Provenance	Museum Description
4	2003-269	Kirklees Museums and Galleries	Unprovenanced	Bird Mummy
5	15895	Kirklees Museums and Galleries	Saft el-Henna, 22nd-26th Dynasty	Crocodile Mummy
6	KMA 1993.250	Kendal Museum	Unprovenanced	Hawk Mummy
17	Ha6357	Bristol Museum and Art Gallery	Beni Hasan	Cat Mummy
19	Ha6356	Bristol Museum and Art Gallery	Beni Hasan	Cat Mummy
27	E5408	Garstang Museum, University of Liverpool	Unprovenanced	Hawk Mummy
29	'Chester Mummy'	Garstang Museum, University of Liverpool	Late Period	Cat mummy
32	E5704a	Garstang Museum, University of Liverpool	Esna?	Fish Mummy
50	11295	Manchester Museum	Ptolemaic Period?	Hawk Mummy
51	1971.21	Manchester Museum	North Saqqara, Ptolemaic Period	Hawk Mummy
54	4295	Manchester Museum	Unprovenanced	Hawk Mummy
55	6098	Manchester Museum	Abydos	Ibis Mummy
56	11501	Manchester Museum	Saqqara	Ibis Mummy
60	12015	Manchester Museum	Beni Hasan	Cat head
62	A957	Manchester Museum	Unprovenanced	Cat Mummy
65	563	Manchester Museum	Gurob	Dog Mummy
68	EA19/2	Manchester Museum	Hawara, Roman Period	Crocodile Mummy
70	1772	Manchester Museum	Unprovenanced	Crocodile Mummy
71	12008	Manchester Museum	Ptolemaic Period?	Crocodile Mummy
76	6033	Manchester Museum	Bought at Aswan	Shrew Mummy
78	6293	Manchester Museum	Beni Hasan, 22nd Dynasty	Cat Mummy
82	6034	Manchester Museum	Unprovenanced	Dog Mummy
88	11296	Manchester Museum	Ptolemaic Period?	Ibis Mummy
108	1.1983.?	Bolton Museum and Art Gallery	Unprovenanced	Fish Mummy
149	J31.5.78.18	Museums Sheffield	Unprovenanced	Ibis/Cat Mummy
150	DBYMU1929-189/1	Derby Museum	Unprovenanced	Cat Mummy
154	137/1993/2	Royal Albert Memorial Museum, Exeter	Unprovenanced	Hawk Mummy
161	TWCMS:2001.406	Sunderland Museum	Unprovenanced	Jackal Mummy
162	EG727	Oriental Museum, Durham	Roman Period	Ibis Mummy in Stone Coffin
174	EG726	Oriental Museum, Durham	Saqqara?, Roman Period	Jackal Mummy
180	9303a-b	Manchester Museum	Ptolemaic Period	Cat Mummy and Coffin
203	1864 HE.21	Old Speech Room Gallery, Harrow School	Saqqara	Ibis Mummy
384	6095	Museum of Fine Arts, Boston	Unprovenanced	Bird Mummy
401	6113	Museum of Fine Arts, Boston	Graeco-Roman Period	Animal Mummy
447	1891.36.f	Glasgow Museums	Unprovenanced	Falcon Mummy
454	29.b.1912	Glasgow Museums	Ramesseum, Thebes	Cat Mummy
471	1910.4	Elgin Museum	Unprovenanced	Ibis Mummy?
517	Ibis	Perth and Kinross Museums	Saqqara? Late-Roman Period	Ibis Mummy
596	Sekhmet Statuette and Mummy	Plymouth City Museum	Unprovenanced	Bronze Votive Statuette of Sekhmet
652	16.11.06.158	World Museum, Liverpool	Esna	Fish Mummy
734	42.18.2	World Museum, Liverpool	Early Roman Period	Cat Mummy
743	M14289	World Museum, Liverpool	Unprovenanced	Crocodile Mummy
764	A.2007.1.10	Glasgow Museums	Unprovenanced	Unwrapped Cat Head
765	A.2007.1.12	Glasgow Museums	Unprovenanced	Hawk Mummy
784	UC30690	Petrie Museum, UCL	Saqqara, 30th Dynasty	Ibis Mummy
791	UC30693	Petrie Museum, UCL	Saqqara, 30th Dynasty	Ibis Mummy